Andrea:
Thanks for
my sis! All the best

MW01355647

LAUGHING ALL THE WAY

The Christmas Letters

John J. Post
©2015

ACKNOWLEDGEMENTS

For providing so much love and such original material for this book, I'd like to thank my best friend and wife, Rana, and my super sons, Canton and Harper. Montana the dog and Annabelle the beast were also helpful.

For loving me and believing that I can do anything (like write a book for instance) and for always encouraging me to dream big: My mom, dad, and sister, Dawn.

I also want to thank the following people for their support (in alphabetical order): the Andersons, Bauers, Goughs, Ladds, and my Willard compatriots.

*Cover art compliments of Becky Treadway.

*Special thanks to Leslie Creath for the cover design.

PROLOGUE 1

I've never written a book before.

The truth is, I thought in order to write a book people would want to read, you had to be famous in some way. But I'm not famous at all. I'm just a middle school English teacher in a small town in Missouri. I have a wife, two kids, and a dog. We live in a house in the suburbs *minus* the white picket fence because I don't know enough about building one to avoid injuring myself or others.

You see, that's the other reason I've never tried to write a book before. I thought that in order to write a book, you not only had to be famous, but you also had to be an *expert* at doing something. I'm an expert at **nothing**. I'm good at some things - like I can swiftly launch an assault on a spider if my wife screams. I can flip back and forth between several sporting events on TV and not get confused. I also write a decently entertaining family Christmas letter.

And that's where this whole book-writing idea came from in the first place.

My friend, Josh, was laughing while reading one of our Christmas letters.

He held up the letter and said, "You need to take these and turn them into a book."

"Uh - how do I turn letters into a book?" I asked.

"I don't know," he said. "I've never written a book." (If you knew him, this wouldn't surprise you.)

"But, how hard could it be?" Josh continued. "It's basically already written."

"Okay - I'll write a book!" I exclaimed. I put my hands on my hips and raised my chin, like a superhero that had just stopped a runaway train.

So as you read this "book" – a woven (and slightly tweaked) compilation of our annual family Christmas letters about marriage, parenting, and just the silliness of life in general, I hope that you will find yourselves (as we have for the past 18+ years) **LAUGHING ALL THE WAY**...

PROLOGUE 2

Plus, how could I ignore these inspiring words hidden inside my fortune cookie?

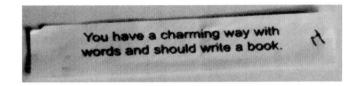

DISCLAIMER

Some of the names in these letters have been changed to avoid any defamation lawsuits that might result from the true (but potentially embarrassing) stories retold here. My wife's name, my kids' names, and the dog's name are their actual names, because I don't think they'd sue me...

CHAPTER ONE
Christmas 1997

The Joys? Of Wedding Planning

Howdy Ya'll (This isn't how we actually talk in Missouri, but I figured "Yule Tidings Ya'll" would sound weird),

Welcome to the first of hopefully many Post Family Christmas letters. I want to apologize up front about the tremendous length of this letter, but we have lots to tell you…

That being said, I guess I should start off with a quick review: last year Rana Bauer agreed to become my fiancé'.

I think the word "fiancé" sounds like the title of a French financial advisor – but that's not what it means at all. What it *really* means is that Rana officially agreed to put up with me for the rest of our lives.

On a snowy evening, I knelt down in front of my apartment and held out the ring.

I yelled, "Will you make me the luckiest man alive and marry me?"

Rana nodded from the doorway with her hands cupped over her mouth. Then, she ran out into the snow (nearly tackling me) before we kissed, hugged, and spun around like frostbitten fools. My upstairs neighbor must have heard the commotion because he opened his door and courtesy-clapped from the balcony.

His clapping made me feel happy. What would **not** make me feel happy was the unexpected mental trauma associated with planning a wedding.

First *seemingly-simple* stop: wedding invitations….On the ride to pick out our invitation, I decided to entertain myself by daydreaming about how my life would be if *I* was forced to work in a wedding invitation store. In order to make the job more bearable, I invented a cute slogan for the store: "We can help you invite em', but we can't make em' show."

My chuckling was interrupted by Rana asking: "So, what do you want our invitations to look like?"

I was kind of startled by the question. To be honest, I didn't care what the invitations looked like – whether they showcased black font, pink glitter font, or sepia tones. (To tell you the absolute truth, until that day, I didn't even know sepia was a color. I would have guessed it was some sort of foot fungus.) Invitations mailed or sent in magnet form. It didn't matter to me. To include or not include that little piece of waxy-paper called vellum. ('Intestinal parasite' would have been my guess for the meaning of the word "vellum.")

I said: "Hon, it really doesn't matter to me what the invitations look like."

"It *doesn't matter* to you?" she asked, wrinkling her brow.

(I'll admit, the phrase "doesn't matter" sounded *much* worse out loud than it did in my head. The rest of the car ride was relatively silent.)

I finally found the invitation place and we entered, a tiny bell announcing our arrival. A super-smiley woman greeted us and led us into a side room with a huge circular oak table. There was a leaning tower of approximately 13,000 wedding invitations erected on that table. I gasped in horror. Rana gasped like she had just won Powerball.

I sat down stiffly. I was afraid if I bumped the table, the tower would collapse and kill me.

The invitation lady told us to take our time in picking out the *perfect* invitation and then headed out of the room.

I mumbled, "Hurry back if you hear a crash."

Rana sat down next to me and picked up twenty invitations from the top of the pile. I tensed up waiting for an avalanche of love paper. The structure swayed slightly.

For the next hour, I watched Rana's hands blur through the invitations like a veteran Las Vegas card dealer – until she was left with 25 "finalists." Then, she began to fan through those carefully until her eyes locked onto one.

Her eyes sparkled as she picked up the invitation and said, "I've found the one."

"And so have I," I replied and kissed her cheek. (I felt witty.)

Well, that was relatively painless I thought happily as I stood up from the chair.

Rana took my arm and said, "Oh, we aren't done. We have *lots* to decide about this invitation… Like, should our invitation say, 'request the honour of your presence' or 'request the honor of your presence'?"

"I don't get the difference," I said, sitting back down.

She answered, "Well, I like honour with the 'ou' because it looks fancier. Like, I'd rather eat lunch at a sandwich shoppe with an 'e' on the word shoppe, than a sandwich shop with no 'e'. I also like when marquees spell 'theater' like 'theatre' with the 'r-e' at the end."

"Are we getting married in England?" I asked.

She stared at me. I cleared my throat and said, "Go with the 'ou' spelling."

She smiled and then said, "Great… And - do we want that little card inside the envelope to say, 'Mr. and Ms._____ will be able to attend' and then below it have, 'Mr. and Ms._____ regretfully cannot attend'"?

I mistakenly said, "Babe, I don't want to put words in people's mouths with that whole 'regretfully cannot attend' thing."

"What do you mean?" she asked.

"Well, what if – hypothetically - the person receiving our invitation hates having plans that take up their Saturday? What if the blank line that says, 'regretfully cannot attend' doesn't reflect their *actual* attitude about not attending? What if, *in reality*, they're thinking: 'I'm *thrilled* to not be attending that wedding.'"

"That isn't a very loving thing to be thinking about," she wrinkled her brow.

"Uh… Er… Uh…" Then, thankfully, an idea hit me.

I took Rana's hand. "Look, I want you to be happy," I said. "I want you to pick *any* invitation - any color, size, font style, word choice - regardless of price - that makes you feel everlasting love, okay?"

She hugged me tightly. (That was easy. Why on earth couldn't I have come up with that line the moment we sat down???)

I felt like I was on a roll so I volunteered to buy stamps for the invitations.

"What kind of stamps are you going to buy?" she asked.

"The kind you don't have to lick?" I shrugged.

"I mean what kind of *picture* will be on the stamps?" she wanted to know.

"What about Liberty Bell stamps?" I suggested. "Then people might think of wedding bells." (I was actually proud of the connection I made there.)

"Absolutely not!" Rana stood up from her chair. "There's a crack on the Liberty Bell. Our marriage will be strong, not cracked. Plus, crack is a dangerous drug."

I stared at her.

"The stamps have to be love-themed *and* be pretty," she sighed.

"Okay," I continued. "What about tropical fishes from the Caribbean or something? Those are pretty."

"Are you insane?! Fish have mercury in them. Mercury poisoning is responsible for hundreds of human deaths each year. Plus, there's Freddie Mercury. Hello?! We can't have people thinking about deceased musicians dressed as shirtless construction workers before our wedding."

"Fine - *you* get the stamps," I said, throwing up my hands.

"Okay," she agreed. "And don't forget we're looking at wedding cakes next Saturday."

Oh fun. (For you curious people, after *several* hours, we settled on white cake with white butter cream frosting and dainty white icing flowers. I vetoed the plastic-looking icing called "fondant." For starters, I thought 'fondant' sounded too much like another foot fungus.)

But *choosing* the invitations and cake was just the beginning of the exhausting wedding process. There was selecting our wedding colors: meticulously cross-referencing flower colors, bridesmaid dress colors, and church carpet and tile colors. (My color blindness made this difficult.) And once all the color schemes finally came together (I think?) and we reserved the church, limo, photographer, and hotel reception, I had to spend an inordinate amount of time trying to convince our DJ that we honestly did NOT want him to play the song "YMCA" at our reception.

But good news was on the way. Rana told me that we needed to register for gifts. Now this was something I could really sink my teeth into! I love gifts. They make me happy. (Almost happy enough to bounce up and down with my arms raised in YMCA letters - but not quite.)

First, we had to decide where to register. My choice was Football World. This idea got sacked quickly. Instead, we headed to a bed and bath store. When we arrived at the counter, the manager armed my fiancé with a gift registry LRT gun. The manager demonstrated how the gun worked on an innocent blender. He pointed the gun at the barcode on the blender, pulled the "trigger," and we heard a beeping sound. This meant the item had been successfully registered.

"Pretty simple," he said. (I nodded in agreement. This *had* to be simpler than picking out wedding invitations.)

My fiancé wanted to operate the LRT first. I was okay with that because I'm afraid of guns.

"Do you like this?" Rana asked, pointing at a stunning liquid soap pump.

"Sure," I half-shrugged.

"Let's register for it," she said.

"Ok, fire when ready," I said. (See: "Bad Gift Registry Jokes," page 1…)

She slowly raised the gun to the soap dispenser and squinted like Clint Eastwood. She was ready to shoot, but her finger was hesitant. Finally, she pulled the trigger. Beep, beep, beep!

She giggled and I gave her a high five.

Then, the fever hit quickly. Within 4 seconds, Rana went from timid shooter to a decorated member of S.W.A.T.

She ducked behind the dinner plates and leapt out and fired at a stack of placemats. The placemats didn't move and beeping erupted from the LRT. She turned and shot 4 bar stools, with her eyes closed. Beep, beep, beep! She then flashed by me, executed a full-aisle body roll, and came out of it on one knee only to fire at a pair of unarmed pillowcases. There was so much beeping going off that I felt like I was in a casino.

"We're winning, we're winning!" I hollered.

She grinned and continued to fire at hyper speed.

I told her I thought she shot the bath towels too many times. She ignored me and kept firing.

Within 20 minutes, Rana had registered us for so many gifts, that we would have had to invite all of England in order to get them all. (And I'm pretty positive she didn't buy that many stamps.)

The dilemma of gift registry for men is that, like the wedding invitations, most of us don't really care. What will our dinner glasses look like? It doesn't matter, unless those dinner glasses are called pilsners. Or steins.

This is why it hurt so deeply that when I finally *did* show an interest in an item, my idea got brushed to the side. (For informational purposes, the item I fell in love with was a shower head the size of a tractor's back tire. It was called The Swedish Tsunami.)

"That's the biggest shower head I've ever seen," Rana said. "We could drown."

I told her that was precisely why it was cool enough to buy.

We looked at the price and saw it was $175. This created a whole other issue: What is the price ceiling of a single item for which to register? When does registering for a certain item become a violation of basic wedding gift registry etiquette? Is it $100? $200? $5,632?

You don't want the people you're inviting to your wedding to get to the store, look at the registry list, and say, "Are they joking?! Those jerks expect us to buy them this over-priced, fancy-

19

pants shower head?! That's it! I'm not wasting five hours of my Saturday at their wedding!"

But in the end it didn't matter.

Strangely, our LRT gun had run out of battery power…

In spite of the fact that my best (?) man locked my wedding ring in his car an hour before the big event, the wedding was truly lovely. As I stood on the altar waiting for the wedding to start, I scanned the crowd and noticed that most of the people we invited showed up – so those perfect invitations must have worked like a charm. Then, the music began playing, the back doors of the church opened, and I saw Rana walking down the aisle carrying white calla lilies. I could hardly breathe, and I couldn't stop smiling… And it must have been a very touching ceremony since I cried and was barely able to get through my wedding vows.

A few minutes later, the priest smiled and told me I could kiss the bride. I did – without crying. There was cheering as we walked arm-in-arm toward the doors of the church, and I knew this was going to be the beginning of something amazing.…

Well, this letter has gone on longer than it should… But I wanted to end with a quote. It was on a sign that we saw while driving recently. We passed an old run-down looking restaurant in the middle of nowhere (actually if you're living in Missouri, that isn't very specific.) Anyway, a flashing sign caught our eye: "EAT HERE OR WE'LL BOTH STARVE."

We had to smile, because it really hit home how dependent we are on each other for love, support, (and even wedding planning). We lean on each other in times of struggle and rejoice with each other in times of celebration. We are truly sustained by our family and friends. Thinking of this made us very thankful for all of you and everything you've added to our lives.

So, may this holiday season be a time when we continue to count the blessings of the friends we have, and recognize, with grateful hearts, all they do to make us whole.

Love and prayers,

John and Rana (aka: The Posts)

CHAPTER TWO
Christmas 1998

Honeymoon Phase and Home-Buying

.

Dear Friends (I was going to write "Dear friends *and* family," but then it occurred to me, that might suggest that if you're our family, you're *not* our friends. I don't agree with that at all, so I just stuck with "Dear Friends," - in case you're the curious type.),

I have to tell you, this marriage thing has been pretty outstanding.

Recently one morning, it hit me that Rana was (hopefully) the last girl I would wake up next to for the rest of my life. In spite of each of us sporting crazy-bed hair, miserable morning breath, and pillow-creased cheeks, I was genuinely happy to be laying there beginning our journey together.

"Good morning, awesome husband," she said.

"Good morning, beautiful wife," I replied.

And we just lay there and grinned at each other like idiots.

She said, "Let me make breakfast for you."

"No, let me!" I insisted.

"I love you!" I hollered.

"I love you more!" she hollered back.

And we wrestled and laughed until we realized it would be more fun to make breakfast together. (Maybe naked.)

They call this the Honeymoon Phase... It is a magical dimension where acting like you truly are, is encouraged and even enjoyed by your significant other. Luckily, Rana and I are still deeply entrenched in it. Examples:

Me to Rana: "The meals you 'cook' typically taste like charcoal briquettes. But that's okay. Water can wash down almost anything – and I love you passionately."

Rana to me: "You cannot handle the most basic tools without injuring yourself or others, but depending on their placement, some scars can be sexy - and I adore you."

Me to Rana: "You operate your motor vehicle like a visually impaired New York cab driver. However, I will *gladly* ride with you now that my dental insurance has been updated – plus, I think you're enchanting."

But our married friends have told us that time will slowly eat away at the Honeymoon Phase. And the things you once found fascinating and charming about your partner will begin to lose a little luster. Friends tell us that the previous comments about cooking, tool handiness, and driving will eventually sound like this:

Me to Rana: "How in the world can you make macaroni and cheese out of a box taste like it was scraped from the bottom of the grill? I couldn't wash this down with molten lava!"

Or…

Rana to Me: "You stuck the screwdriver *where*?! Well, you better dial 9-1-1, because riding in a speeding ambulance is *a lot safer* than driving with *me*, isn't it?!"

Thank goodness, that isn't us…yet?

So, we took advantage of still being immersed in this Honeymoon Phase, by spending our actual honeymoon in the romantic city of San Francisco. It was breathtaking – literally. See, I was still on crutches from having knee surgery and San Francisco has been nicknamed "The City of Enormous Hills." (Actually that's not true. I think its real nickname has something to do with inescapable island prisons, but the point is, the hills there *are* insanely steep!) In spite of major arm-pit discomfort during most of our exploring, Rana and I seemed to fall even further in love in the midst of the most gorgeous city we had ever seen. We plan to go back one day – minus the crutches, if possible.

Then, something *really* exciting happened a few days after we returned home from our honeymoon. I was outside getting the mail. (I know *that's* not very exciting. Be patient.) I pulled down the mailbox door and peered inside. Dang it. The mailman forgot to repay the $1.2 million dollars I loaned him.

I shrugged and pulled out a stack of bills. And peeking out between the bills...

Oh! What's this? A colorful postcard? I held it closer for inspection. It read: "YOU too can be a homeowner!" (There was a picture of a Malibu mansion over-looking the ocean.) I flipped the card over, and found, that with a mere 10% down, we could join the rest of the planet in home ownership.

I crutched myself into the duplex we were renting and called out to Rana: "Honey! Come see this!"

"You already showed me how you can flex one butt cheek at a time," she called back.

"No, not that!" I yelled. "I wanna' build a house!"

I heard laughing coming from the back room.

"*You* can't build a *house*," she said coming down the hall. "Sweetie, you can barely change the batteries in the smoke detectors." (Honeymoon Phase nearing an early end?)

I was insulted. "*I'm* not going to build it," I said. "This company is." I handed her the card.

Rana was intrigued. The idea of not hearing our neighbors through the bedroom wall was fascinating.

We sat down at the kitchen table and began implementing a money saving plan. Step #1: Stop eating out every night... This wasn't going to be easy.

27

We were approximately 100% short of the required 10% down payment due to the fact that we had blown through all our wedding dough in San Fran. On the plus side, thanks to my wife's itchy gift registry trigger finger, we did have enough bath towels to dry the entire island of Cuba.

Immediately, we started stashing every spare cent for a six month stretch. We traded in CDs. We kept the A/C off. We cut the cable TV. We sold clothes (and stacks of towels) at the resale shop. We ate every meal at home. Coincidentally, this was around the time Ramen Noodle Co. officially announced that three of their top executives were retiring because of "the generous patronage of a delightful couple from Missouri."

Even though we were saving most of our money, we did splurge on a book called, *Home Buying for Dummies*. Right off the bat, we both acknowledged that this book was awarding us **far too many** IQ points. We read the book together each night and learned about crucial phrases such as: "escrow accounts," "fixed and variable rates," and "building a home can kill you."

Then, we met with the loan officer who went over our credit history. His eyes were scanning his computer monitor and then locked onto something. He looked up at me and smiled.

He said, "So John, you have a $5,500 credit card balance at Fashion Gal – the *ladies'* clothing store?"

My wife looked at me in disbelief. "You shop at *Fashion Gal?*!" (Honeymoon Phase O-V-E-R.)

I shook my head (vigorously).

The problem was that it was that delinquent Fashion Gal account that had my credit score located somewhere near Hades and was keeping us from qualifying for the home loan. It turned out some lady who went by the alias No-Pay Charlene had stolen my social security number and opened the account. Sadly, No-Pay

Charlene was not interested in making payments on this account. It now became my job to convince the Credit Bureau, the FBI, and the Pope that the loan was opened fraudulently.

Anyway, after a truckload of paperwork (and what may have been a colonoscopy) I finally proved that it wasn't me who opened the account at the ladies' clothing store, Fashion Gal. This saved both money and my masculinity. Finally, we qualified for the home loan.

On another positive side note, No-Pay Charlene got caught. Apparently she was going to be locked up for a while since she was charged in 16 other cases of identity theft across the country…We were happy…Because, as the old, familiar saying goes, "Identity thieves should be forced to eat prison food for a long time."

After getting approved for the loan, we started waiting for the builders to *do something*. We drove to our new neighborhood each night to check on our lot. I can't explain our jubilation when we arrived one night and saw a hole. It was a gigantic rectangular hole in the ground. We stood in it and held each other tightly. This hole was going to be our home!

I visited the builders regularly – much to their irritation. I began to notice things that I wanted changed. I mentioned them to the builder. He told me load bearing walls could not be moved – especially after they were already in place. I asked if they could "tweak" the way the fireplace had been framed. I told him that I had seen his men work and I was confident they could do *anything*. My confidence was rewarded with a pencil drawing of a middle finger nailed to the newly framed fireplace. I got the message and stopped visiting (as much).

The house finally got finished, the inspector checked things out, and then came the final step called *Closing*. I think Closing shouldn't be called Closing. It should be called *Signing*. We signed our names on so many forms that the last ones didn't even look like our signatures. My wife and I then initialed the final form which stated that if we defaulted on the loan, the bank would arrange for us to be cell-mates with No-Pay Charlene. Then the loan lady handed us the keys to our house. There were hugs. The builder was there and he even shook my hand. This made me feel good. Then, it was time to move in.

As my buddies and I lugged in the heavy furniture and over-stuffed boxes, Rana and her mom focused on getting the kitchen set up. Where should the bowls go? And the cups? Which drawer should hold the silverware? At the time, my wife felt these decisions were of unparalleled importance. What would happen, for example, if the salad plates' position in the upper cabinet to the right of the dishwasher, felt awkward?

Our "help" finally headed home after eating pizza out of a box and my wife and I collapsed on the floor. We couldn't wait to take a shower and sleep. But that wasn't going to happen because Hurricane Holy-Crappola rolled in and began tattooing all four sides of our house. Ordinarily, this wouldn't have been a problem except that the builders "forgot" to put seals around the back French door and had "accidentally" put our living room windows in upside down causing them not to seal at all. (How did I miss all of this upon my meticulous inspections?!)

Well, I'm not sure how Noah handled the whole flood thing, but we handled it with hyperventilation. Rain water was literally pouring through the door in our kitchen and windows into our living room. Our only choice was to pile the few towels we had left like sand bags to sop up the water. Of course, our new dryer outlet was not compatible with our old dryer, so we were forced to hand-wring the sopping towels in the sink until 2 AM.

Just before the storm ended, I had the brilliant idea. Using a butter knife (which, by the way, took me *way* too long to find due to its placement in a drawer that made absolutely NO SENSE), I smashed plastic shopping bags into the gaping seal around the door. (Who's not handy?) By the time I was done mushing, I couldn't

30

even open the door. But it did stop the water... Everything eventually dried out, and we are loving our new home.

Aside from home building, a lot has changed in our careers. Rana used to work two jobs. First, she was a part time Child Life Specialist at the local hospital helping kids and parents deal with the hospital experience. In addition, Rana was also a part time nanny for three-year-old twin boys.

The only problem with the Child Life job was that, although she loved it, she worked many nights and most weekends. The problem with the nanny job was that the only time Rana left the twins alone with me, one of them pooped in his pants at McDonald's. This was hard for all.

Then, nearly out of the blue, Rana's boss at the hospital resigned, and Rana was asked to become the new Child Life coordinator full time. What a blessing since now she doesn't work weekends or nights and we get to spend a lot more time together (which we actually still enjoy).

In terms of my career, I love teaching 7th and 8th grade Language Arts and coaching middle school football and track. Sometimes teaching grammar can be tough – but I have yet to have any of my students have an accident in their pants – so it sure beats being a nanny-assistant.

Well, I'm pooped (sorry, couldn't resist) so I better wrap this up...

I heard something funny from my sister-in-law, Marsha, recently as we discussed Rana and I being newly married. Marsha told me that she knew an elderly gentleman who had been married nearly 50 years. He was always smiling and loved to tell the following joke:

"The first few years of marriage to your wife, you just wanna' eat em' up… The last few years of marriage, you wish you had."

I laughed when I heard this – partly because it was hilarious – and partly because I cannot imagine the years ever fading the feelings Rana and I have for each other.

So, as we reflect back on 1998, we'd like to offer you our prayers for your upcoming year: May your credit remain unstolen, may your home be filled with love and properly installed windows, may all your silverware reside in the most conveniently-located drawers… But most importantly, we pray that you can linger awhile with the ones you love in that place they call the Honeymoon Phase.

All our love and prayers,

John, Rana, (And No-Pay Charlene, wherever she is)

CHAPTER THREE
Christmas 1999

The Marriage Playbook, Football Lessons & Our "First" Halloween

34

Dearest Loved Ones,

(Upon re-reading that greeting, the word "loved" sounds like it is the past tense of "love." So, we want you to know that the love we have for you is very much currently happening, and not expired.)

Last year, Rana and I were so wiped out from the house-building process that we didn't even put up a Christmas tree. This year, we decided to stop being lame. So, last evening, Rana and I finished "erecting" our first *live* Christmas tree and, more importantly, neither of us filed for divorce. It was an epic saga, however: husband and wife struggling beneath a sticky, sap-ridden, pine-needle-dropping, naughty- language-inducing green monster, trying to make a tree that has no problem standing straight on the side of a mountain, stand straight in a carpeted living room. But we did it!

Rana then hurried me toward the study where the computer awaited me. It was time to write this year's Christmas letter... My failing grades in "Gift Wrapping 101" originally forced me into this annual responsibility since I was once told my gift wrapped present looked like it was done by someone without fingers.

So here we go... In last year's Christmas letter, I mentioned that Rana and I became first time home owners. And let me tell you, first time homeownership is exciting. There is a tremendous feeling of accomplishment. But the one downside of it for a married couple is that this is the first time all aspects of home maintenance fall on both of you. There's no landlord to call when the A/C goes out or when you can't seem to figure out how to get the smoke detectors to stop chirping. There's no duplex company that slides in to clear the snow from your sidewalk. Truthfully, homeownership forces a husband and wife to look around their giant investment and decide who is going to do what and how often they are going to do it.

In last year's letter, I also mentioned that Rana and I were still enjoying the Honeymoon Phase of our marriage. And while no one knows the exact cause of the Honeymoon Phase ending, a recent clinical study determined the end might directly correlate with the moment a husband and wife attempt to discuss who "does more" around the house.

Example: I walked into the house after mowing the lawn. I was sweaty. I had cut grass stuck to my legs and arms. I didn't smell good. And I was hungry.

My clean wife was lying on the couch, reading a book. She looked very comfortable and very not interested in moving.

"What's for dinner?" I asked, wiping my brow.

"I don't know," she replied without looking up. "I hadn't really thought about it."

I wiped my brow in a much more exaggerated fashion. She looked up - unimpressed by my sweat or apparent fatigue.

She said, "What do you feel like making?"

(In my head: *What do I feel like making? I feel like making you put down that sloppy romance novel so you can make me a sandwich – or order us a pizza – whichever is intestinally safer.*)

What I actually said *out loud* was much better: "Uh, I kinda thought you might take care of dinner since I just mowed the yard."

She looked surprised - but in a slightly irritated way.

"Well, I cleaned our bathroom this morning," she said. "So I thought you'd do the cooking tonight."

I said, "Wiping your toothpaste spit off the faucet is not cleaning. It's called common courtesy."

"I washed three loads of your clothes yesterday," she said, sitting up on the couch.

"I just mowed the yard!" I reminded her, pointing down at my grassy legs.

She shook her head. "Mowing the yard isn't a chore," she said. "You *like* mowing the yard."

"I don't *like* mowing the yard. I mow because I'm afraid you'll cut your foot off..."

I need to interrupt this story to provide you readers with some pertinent information: There's an old saying that goes: "Even when a man is right, he's wrong." I don't know who said that phrase but it might have been Jesus.

The existence of this phrase caused Man to create the Marriage Playbook. Men spend most of their lives trying to master it. With a little practice, many of the plays are simple enough to be run successfully by even the most intelligence-challenged man. The most basic, fundamental of these plays is called the "Of Course I'm Wrong Because You Are Right" play. When executed with sincerity, it has a 99.9% success rate. Most men decide they need to master this play within the first 14 hours of marriage.

But the most difficult and daring of all man-plays in the Marriage Playbook appears on the last page. This play is so daring and difficult, that there is no record of this play ever being run successfully. Sadly, some men have lost their lives attempting to run this play. It's called the "I'm Going To Compare What I Do Around the House To What You Do Around The House In Order To Prove I Do More" play.

As I stared at my wife on the couch, I was faced with a decision: Run the most fundamental play in the playbook, or ignore statistics and attempt the play from the last page. The choice seemed obvious.

I said it: "I think you should cook dinner tonight because - I mean, let's be honest - I do A LOT more around this house than you do." (I realize in the long history of man, there have likely been MUCH smoother attempts at running this play.)

Rana ~~set~~ slammed her book down on the coffee table and stood up: "Uh – have you forgotten I do ALL of your laundry."

"I do ALL the outside yard work," I said.

"I unload the dishwasher," she said. "And I clean the toilets because ever since that McDonald's incident, you've been afraid of other people's poop germs."

She squinted. I squinted. (I thought I saw a tumbleweed roll by.) There was no flinching in this Wild (Mid)-West showdown.

She then craftily brought the standoff to an abrupt halt: "We *WERE* going to have some *fun* tonight, if you know what I mean."

"You like your steak medium, right?" I asked and headed out to the grill...

Truthfully, Rana and I don't argue very often. In a marriage, we've quickly discovered that marital happiness is directly related to compromise and the ability to appreciate the likes of the other spouse. In saying that, I'm pretty sure Rana should get a lifetime achievement award for how dramatically she transformed her attitude about the viewing of televised sports.

I remember it was a Sunday. That meant two things: God in the morning, football in the afternoon.

I was flopped on the couch flipping back and forth between two football games. (It's amazing that in everyday life when I'm trying to do two different things at once, I struggle. But watching two different football games simultaneously doesn't confuse me in the slightest.)

38

My wife sat down next to me. As I switched the channel every 30 seconds, she blinked in confusion.

"Can I watch too?" she asked.

"You wanna watch *football?*" I asked, looking at her sideways. "I thought you didn't like it?"

"Well, I know you love it so decided I wanted to learn about it."

"That's awesome," I smiled and put my arm around her shoulder.

We watched for about ten minutes. I kept it on one channel as not to confuse her. (I'm considerate.)

At one point I shouted something naughty at the TV. She was startled, but stayed seated.

Suddenly, she crinkled her nose, pointed to the TV, and said, "I don't like that team's outfits."

"*Outfits?*" I chuckled.

"Yeah, the outfits they're wearing," she re-affirmed.

"Those are called *uniforms,*" I said.

She said, "Okay." And after a pause said, "And why does the guy with the ball just run into the big pile of guys in front of him?"

"Well, the guys in front of him are supposed to make a hole for him to run through."

"I haven't seen any hole since I've been watching," she said.

"That's why I cussed earlier," I said.

She turned to me and said, "Look. I never knew they were supposed to make a hole. That was good information to know. So when we're watching, if you think something important is happening, you tell me what it is. I'll learn that way."

Thus, the training began. Like Mr. Miagi and the Karate Kid. Yoda and Luke Skywalker…If there was a game on, we watched it. Afternoon or evening. Early kickoff or late. We were tuned in.

I dissected each play - actually going up to the TV and using my finger to analyze offensive and defensive formations. I explained penalties, why the refs wore stripes, and why the football was strangely shaped. I explained the evolution of the football helmet – from leather to plastic –while discussing the importance of other protective gear such as shoulder pads, thigh pads, and cup.

And she seemed to be absorbing it all. Quickly.

A few weeks later, we were watching another game together. On one play, a receiver got bumped while going up for a pass.

I jumped up from the couch and yelled, "Where's the flag for pass interference?!"

Rana gently patted my arm and said, "No Hon, I think that was *incidental contact*."

Dear God, what have I done?

That was last year… This year, my teaching buddy Ronny and I decided to go head to head in a football pool. The object was simple: Pick the winner of one game each week, never picking the same team to win or lose more than twice during the season. The person with the best record at the end of the season cooked the other's family a full-fledged BBQ with no restrictions on menu or spirits. Sounds fun, huh? I went home and off-handedly mentioned it to Rana.

She said, "I wanna' play."

Next day at school I asked Ronny. He laughed, "Isn't this the same girl who referred to the NFL uniform as an *outfit*?"

"Yeah, but she's really been -"

"Let her play. It'll be fun."

("It'll be fun," also happens to be the most frequently uttered sentence on the Titanic prior to leaving the dock.)

I'll cut to the chase. Ronny and I got knocked out of the pool halfway through the season. My wife never lost a game. Consequently, Rana requested her filet be grilled medium rare and her Moscato, chilled.

As he chewed, Ronny pointed his fork at Rana and said, "You're not allowed to play with next year."

Rana just smiled. And honestly, I did too. I was pretty proud of her.

And my pride has continued to grow with each passing day – except for a small hiccup during Halloween - when I learned something *shocking* about this woman I thought I knew so well. Please allow me to explain...

Back when we lived in our duplex, there weren't many kids who lived in our neighborhood. Therefore, when Halloween rolled around, we just decided "to not be home" when little goblins came lurking up to our door. Well, this past year, we decided we needed to participate in the spooky holiday like the rest of America.

And my wife was so jazzed up to *truly* be celebrating our "first" Halloween that she purchased $195 worth of candy.

"This is a *big* neighborhood," she explained.

41

For those who have never really thought about it, couples basically have two roles during Halloween. You have the "Candy Giver" and you have the "Person Standing Behind the Candy Giver Who Comments About Each Costume." Rana wanted to be the "Candy Giver" and I was okay with that.

Anyway, I kind of stood back and observed her each time the doorbell rang. ***And this is when I found out the shocking TRUTH:***

My wife is a Costume (and Age) Discriminator. The amount of candy she gave was directly related to the "cuteness" of the trick or treater's costume and even the trick or treater's age. In other words, if you were a teenager going as a "teenager," you might as well not have knocked on our door. Into your bag, my wife tossed raisins and a pamphlet entitled, "Yes – You're Too Old to Trick or Treat."

But if you were cute. And a toddler. And perhaps a little chubby and dressed like a koala bear...Mercy. My wife unloaded 31 Snickers bars on you... One girl – who was wearing a Dorothy costume – was barely able to drag her overflowing bag off our porch as she waddled away in her ruby slippers yelling, "Enough! Enough!"

After Halloween, Rana and I took a much-needed trip to Orlando, Florida to attend a childhood friend's wedding. Luckily, the Best Man from my own wedding, Cool Chris, was a pilot also living near Orlando. After the wedding, Cool Chris picked us up in his private plane. He then flew us to Jupiter (the city, not the planet. Because that would make Cool Chris an astronaut, not a pilot...) My grandma, who also happens to live near Jupiter, (again the city, not planet because that would make my grandma an alien) lent us her private beach pass, and we spent the entire glorious afternoon, relaxing on the beach - Rana soaking in the rays and watching the ocean while Cool Chris and I played "fishermen" for the day – even tugging in a three foot Moray Eel off the rock jetty. I mention this trip because Rana and I realized then and there: We'd love to retire near the beach one day if at all possible. (That's if our careers will allow it, of course.)

Speaking of our careers... Rana's still at the hospital running the Child Life department as smoothly as ever and has even picked up a few teaching gigs at the local college.

It's also been an interesting year for me. A day after taking a CPR class at school, I saved a boy in our cafeteria who was choking on a whole chicken nugget .... As a silly side note, I wasn't able to save our football season. We finished 0-5-1 and I knew it was bad when, at the end of one game, the head coach of the opposing team greeted me on the field with, "Man, I'm soooo sorry."

And *I* should probably say sorry for making this letter so long.

But I'm more than capable of saying sorry. In fact, saying "sorry" is on the second page of *The Marriage Playbook*...

And – in closing – I'll mention one more excerpt from the Marriage Playbook that will hopefully get you ready for next year's letter. Somewhere toward the middle of the book is a chapter entitled "Strengthening Your Team." This chapter involves a couple's choice to add a little life to their marriage - and I'm not talking about drinking margaritas in excess. Instead, I'm referring to the moment a couple decides they are ready to share their love for each other – with a little baby. Rana and I have recently arrived at this chapter and we're excited about the possibilities ahead.

As always, we'll keep you Posted. (Pardon the pitiful pun.)

Love and prayers,

The two Posts (And maybe soon to be 3?)

44

CHAPTER FOUR
Christmas 2000

*The Trials and Tribulations of
First-Time Pregnancy*

H oly News-Filled Christmas Letter, Batman,

So I'll start with the BIGGEST (or tiniest) news first. For anyone who doesn't know yet, we're going to have a baby. Though, I guess the word "we" is a bit misleading. *My* belly won't be protruding - causing me to unintentionally knock over table lamps and small children. Rana will take care of that.

The funny thing about this pregnancy is that it seems to have followed one of those weird rules of the universe - the harder you try for something, the longer it feels like it takes to achieve it. We were trying so hard, (no, I'm not complaining) but weren't getting pregnant. So, a friend suggested getting a pet to "mother" to help take our minds off the delay.

During a drive around town, we strategically eliminated the pet possibilities of a bunny, a goldfish, or an elk. Finally, as we passed a Humane Society billboard, we decided we should save a puppy. We walked in with our sanity and left with a 10 week-old, 6 pound Yellow Lab/Golden Retriever mix. We named him Montana, after my childhood hero, Joe Montana. (I'm sure Joe would be flattered.)

So, it was the first full day of puppy ownership. Rana had to be at work. We had stocked up on supplies: chew toys, puppy treats, and doggy diapers (I figured I'd eventually need the practice?)... We also bought two sprays - that to avoid confusion - I shall call, "Pooh and Pee Odor Remover" and "The Pee in This Spot" spray. Obviously the "Pooh and Pee Odor Remover" was designed, in the event of a puppy accident in the house, the smell would be removed. "The Pee in This Spot" spray was designed to be used where we wanted the puppy to go potty on the pee pads, closer and closer to the door, until he'd eventually learn to go potty outside. Rana installed a baby gate to keep Montana (and me) in the kitchen while she was at work. We were ready.

All I know is this. Each time Montana peed or pooped on the kitchen floor, I did as I was supposed to. I wiped it up and blasted the spot with the magic spray. One problem - I was spraying "The Pee in This Spot" spray every place that Montana had gone to the bathroom. (The bottles looked eerily similar.) You can imagine how it was by the afternoon (or maybe you'd rather not), when Montana was sliding around the linoleum floor whizzing pee everywhere - like a spinning garden sprinkler. (Side note: I had also had fed this poor puppy his body weight worth of doggie treats during the day. The box never mentioned a limit. Needless to say, they didn't sit very well with Montana - so it wasn't just pee flying around the kitchen.) Anyway, Mrs. Clean finally came home, figured out my ghastly error, and detoxed the floor. This meant we could eat supper in our kitchen without wearing an aspirator – which would have been tricky... And thankfully, Montana is now a fully potty trained member of our family.

A few months later, I learned we were pregnant. It all happened while I was mowing the yard. (Let me clarify for those having trouble picturing that: the *action* happened earlier in the bedroom. The *news as a result of the action* happened while I was out mowing the yard.)

Rana flagged me down from the doorway. I stopped the mower and walked toward her. She was holding something behind her back. *Please be a chilled beverage*, I thought.

"We're pregnant!" she grinned, and nearly poked out my eye with a pregnancy pee stick.

As soon as the pee stick was no longer a threat to my retina, I hugged her tightly.

"We're gonna' have a babyyyyyyyyy," she said in a cute babyish voice. Then, she did an excited little hop up and down dance move. I hopped with her so she didn't feel left out.

"I have to finish the yard now," I said, and kissed her cheek. "We'll celebrate when I get done and showered."

She said, "Ok," and closed the door, but not before she kissed me again.

I stood there a moment and allowed the news to sink in... My heart was leaping. Then, as I started to push the mower through the yard, my brain went into shock:

...Babies are kinda' sweet like when that famous photographer lady stuffs them in snow peas and watermelons and they look really cute — and maybe a little sticky — but we have those friends who have a new baby and they blab, blab, blab about how cute their baby is, but their baby really resembles a wrinkly troll, so will we become blind to true cuteness when we have a baby too? Can **we** *even afford a baby? How much does Stanford cost? And Yale? And baby food? Can babies survive on Cheerios? Or Cheetos? Oh... Breast milk! That's free. I love free. Hmmmmmm. The whole breast milk thing kinda' freaks me out. I mean, could I accidentally get squirted by the breast milk? Speaking of squirting, I hear there's 100% chance a parent is peed on by their kid while changing their diaper... I wonder if the odds would improve if I could invent a "Pee in This Spot" spray for babies? Man, we shouldn't have donated all those towels from our wedding... We should have kept more than two...Speaking of two, just how bad are the Terrible Twos? And speaking of twos, what if Rana's carrying twins? Or triplets? Or that next big word that means she's having 4 babies at once?!?!*

But in spite of all of the chaos swirling in my head, as I walked the mower into the garage, I couldn't stop smiling. I was still smiling when I caught sight of my two-seater sports car. I was hot, sweaty, covered in grass, and would soon be saying goodbye to that beautiful, black sports car, yet all was right with the world...

Once a doctor visit confirmed that the pee stick was indeed correct, it was time to call *Everyone*. We called our families and they were excited. We then called our friends and their excitement was accompanied by some laughter. They knew our footloose-and-fancy-free lifestyle was about to change drastically. I suppose when we completed our metamorphosis from DINKs (Dual Income No Kids) to DIDDs (Dual Income Down the Drain), we would totally understand what the laughter was all about...

At that point we didn't know if we were having a boy or a girl, yet we did have baby names picked out. We didn't agree on all of them, but Rana kept a running list. However, the name list was TOP SECRET. My wife had this thing about people stealing baby names - like a baby name was an unlocked Mercedes Benz sitting after midnight in the bad part of town. I told Rana that her fear was understandable – since I was named, John, after my father – and obviously my mother stole the name from him. My wife was not amused. To her, baby-name stealing was a felony.

Protecting the names (once you had them) was hard, but picking them out was a nightmare. With the names some celebrities are bludgeoning their own children with these days, you'd think naming your newborn would be as easy as pointing to a random word on a fast food billboard:

"Yep, you heard right, we're naming our baby, Chinabuffet. Unless it's a girl. Then we're naming her Burgerqueen."

So, to help with the process, we bought a *31,000 Baby Names* book. That's not an exaggeration. There really are 31,000 names that exist. (I was shocked too.) Each night we read out loud several hundred unique baby names – many of which didn't sound like they paired very well with our last name. Thus, we wasted valuable time discussing whether or not "Com" or "Goal" could be suitable options.

By the time we bumped "Lamp" off the list, it was time to go in for the Doppler to hear the baby's heartbeat. At first, the whole deal sounded like dolphin sonar under water. (And this worried us since we had eliminated "Flipper" as a baby name possibility weeks before...) But then we heard the pumping beat of our little baby's heart. I remember looking down at my wife and we both squeezed hands tightly. There were eyes welling up too.

Months later came the first ultrasound, and that ultrasound was a pretty amazing event (unless you're scared of petroleum jelly).

"You've got yourselves a little boy," the nurse said, pointing to something on the screen.

I nearly jumped through the ceiling. Rana was happy too, but was lying down and couldn't jump very well. But she was full of smiles…Finally, we could eliminate female names off our Baby Name List.

So, I might as well tell you which name we came up with. Since "Montana" was given to the puppy, I was at a loss. But Rana saved the day by coming up with the idea: Why not name our son after the Ohio city where the Pro Football Hall of Fame was located? Thus, the name Canton, was "born." (And protected with a lockbox and several nuclear warheads.)

Besides baby names, my prep for the baby was coming along pretty slowly. I knew *nothing* about babies. Because of this, my wife signed us up for every baby class offered in the tri-state area. One weekend we attended a class entitled: "Crying a River? No, That's Just Your Wife's Water Breaking." It was a special, special time.

But my "favorite" event might have been the weekend long birthing class we took together. We ended up sitting next to a couple who appeared to have a combined age of 21. The boy was fidgeting in his seat next to me.

There was a matinee video being shown of live childbirth. I'm not sure what the movie was rated, but the lady in the video wasn't wearing any pants. And she was moaning. And she wasn't wearing pants. Normally moaning + buck naked woman = a good thing, but viewing childbirth in stir-ups was as far away from Good Naked as you could get.

I was beginning to squirm in my chair like the kid next to me. Then the lady in the video stopped moaning and began screaming - loudly. A cold sweat was breaking out on my forehead as I looked on in horror. Then, without warning, the baby's head crowned and the doc in the video asked the lady if she wanted to touch her baby. She stopped screaming and reached down between her legs and was rubbing her baby's head as it was protruding from her private place.

The kid next to me mumbled what I think was, "Oh God," and crashed out of the chair like a falling evergreen. He was o-u-t. The instructor hurried over to help the kid. His girlfriend was waving air in his face with her hand. He "came to" and sat up, his head between his knees.

I felt sorry for the kid, and I wanted to be encouraging so I said, "Maybe you could try that Lamaze breathing thing we learned about earlier today."

He looked up and shook his head. Rana jabbed me in the arm with her elbow, but then smiled. I think she was proud that I hadn't passed out because it gave her hope I could be strong during the real deal.

The next weekend, Rana informed me that we got to register for baby presents – just like we got to register for wedding gifts years earlier. This made me excited – and a little nervous. In order to prevent receiving too many of one item (see: bath towels), I asked my wife if I could work the LRT gun. She agreed. But she held the alphabetical list. There was a lot we needed…

I looked over her shoulder at the list. I scanned downed the page. My eyes stopped.

"What are *breast pads*?" I asked.

"I stick them in my bra and they keep breast milk from leaking on my shirt," she said matter-of-factly.

"Your milk is gonna' *leak*?!" I asked, not so matter-of-factly.

52

"Yeah," she said.

I began to think about that.

"Let's not mince words here," I said. "Is it a leak – like a dribble, or a leak – like a *gush*?"

"It's not going to flood our town," she said. "But I hear it can be more than a dribble."

"Really?" I asked.

"Yep," she nodded. "Some books say the milk can *squirt*."

My eyes widened as I thought of something else. I had to ask.

"So," I began, "if I'm standing near you and you don't have a shirt or bra on, and you don't have these breast pads - could your milk squirt in my eye?"

She looked at me.

"I'm serious," I said seriously.

"Uh, I doubt it – unless I grab the back of your head, pull you forward, and squeeze one of my boobs."

I immediately dropped the breast pads discussion and it was then that I noticed the next item on the list was a "breast pump."

I got excited. My wife intercepted my thoughts and said, "Don't get your hopes up. The pump doesn't make them bigger; it pumps breast milk out of them."

"I know," I said. But I didn't really know, obviously. However, I didn't like Rana to know how little I knew about baby stuff. It might send her into early labor...

Rana's belly began to protrude cutely and she felt it was time to prep the house thoroughly prior to Canton's arrival. You see, as first time parents, we (my wife) had an uncanny ability to find the danger-potential in many household items. Honey, peanuts, and uranium had to be removed – end of discussion. And with the removals, also came the safety additions.

I arrived home one day and saw my wife inserting those little plastic covers in each electrical outlet - even in the ones in the backsplash above the kitchen counter.

"Is our newborn going to be 4'6"?" I asked.

"We can't be too careful," she replied.

We put up two foldable baby gates to close off the living room, just in case Canton began running at 6 days old… We had even – on recommendation of the doggy obedience school – recorded the sound of a baby crying so Montana wouldn't go ballistic when hearing it for the first time.

"Young dogs can sometime be aggressive when hearing the distressful sounds of a baby crying – especially if they're hearing them for the first time."

So, we did as we were told. Rana recorded me on a hand-help tape deck crying loudly like a baby. I was VERY convincing. We wrapped the tape recorder up in a baby blanket and put it on the couch and played it. Montana perked up his ears, raised his hackles, then raced to hide under our bed.

So we were all ready(?) Or so I thought… But no man is ever truly ready for the Mood Invader.

When Rana first became pregnant, there were no noticeable side effects. She had a few bouts of morning sickness, but nothing major. Then she started getting her baby bump… And as the baby was getting bigger, it became clear that the baby might be sucking her brain away.

According to my friends who already had babies, their pregnant wives became – what's the word I'm looking for – "sensitive."

"You look gorgeous," I said to my wife one evening.

"You're so sweet," she smiled, then added sheepishly, "but I'm feeling sort of fat."

"I don't think you look fat *at all*," I said convincingly.

She hugged me and whispered, "Ok, then I want a fudge brownie with ice cream for dinner tonight."

"For *dinner?*" I asked (stupidly). "Uh, I'm not sure that's going to help you in terms of feeling fat," I added (stupidly).

"So you **dooooo** think I look like a *cow?!*" she moo – uh, I, mean growled.

"No!" I shook my head emphatically.

"Just admit it," she said, tears beginning to well in her eyes. "You're married to a blubbery whale."

"Where are all these animals coming from?!" I stammered.

Truthfully, we both had been gaining a little weight. That was natural though, according to Dr. Infantile, who was Rana's OB-GYN.

"It's natural for women to gain weight during pregnancy," he said. His statement didn't really phase me until he pointed at me and added, "And the husbands usually gain weight too."

"I'm not gonna' gain any weight," I said to him.

"Yes you will," Dr. Infantile nodded. "I've got two kids. You think I looked like this before I had them?"

I noticed his white doctor coat was a little snug.

My jeans began to get "less comfortable" as we got ready for the first ultrasound…My watch felt a little tight by the 4 month mark.

We went to an appointment at the seven month mark where the doc told Rana she had gained 7 pounds in a week. Rana was angry. Mostly at the doctor.

"I have been eating healthy *and* exercising," Rana insisted. "I think your scale is wrong."

Dr. Infantile was smart and said, "You're right. Our scale must be broken."

That night – perhaps in a tantrum-type state, Rana convinced me to take her to the local greasy diner, for a burger, curly fries, and a chocolate sundae. I thought that sounded great, even though my socks were beginning to cut off the circulation in my swollen ankles.

While we stood in line to place our order, I casually looked to my side and saw Doctor Infantile standing there. I nudged Rana. She looked horrified and his eyes caught hers. She smiled.

He grinned, "Yeah – this is where I go when I'm eating healthy and exercising too."

She leaned into me and whispered, "Order the burger and fries – but don't get the sundae until he leaves."

"You got it," I nodded.

But with all the craziness this pregnancy has brought, there is one thing we're not worried about, and that's daycare. Rana's mom and dad (Myrna Kay and George) have an at-home daycare. This baby is going to get some serious one-on-one attention, and we can't think of anyone we'd rather have watch over our baby!

Besides a new puppy, a new baby on the way, and building a new house with an additional bedroom, this year has been filled with other notable changes. This year I was promoted to head 8th grade football coach. Lots of pressure – especially since last year we didn't win a game. At some point, I joked with the players that if we won four of six games this year, I'd shave my head. Of course as the words came off my lips, I was actually thinking "I'd be happy if we could cross the 50 yard line with some consistency." After we won our first game 32-6, a football mom asked if I was getting ready for my haircut. I smiled politely.

Well, we won our next game, and the next. At the 3-0 juncture, kids in the halls and parents I'd see around town were running their balled-up fists through their hair and making buzzing hair clipper noises. Well I'll be darned if we didn't win game #4 and, as promised, my head was shaved. A parent captured the event on tape - and I know Rana would love to relay the details. Or, maybe you could just borrow the video tape and watch her sobbing in the back of the locker room as players and parents chanted and cheered in euphoria around their way-too-young-to-be-bald football coach.

Well, with your tall beverage(s) probably empty and your eyes begging for this to be done, I better tie this thing up. I'll end with this:

Upon hearing of our pregnancy, a friend said to me, "You've just purchased a new pair of glasses and the world will never look the same." Rana and I were talking about that statement and how nice it sounded. But as we thought about it, we also couldn't imagine the world looking any better than it does now. We've got each other and true love. We've got families that couldn't be more terrific if we had hand- picked them ourselves. We've got the most wonderful friends in the world. And now God has added a little Angel to Rana's tummy.

So, we want to thank each of you, for making up what we see through the "glasses" we wear. You bless us with so many prayers, so much support, and so much love. May God bless you as He has us this holiday season and throughout the coming year.

We love you!

John, Rana, Montana, (and little Angel)

CHAPTER FIVE
Christmas 2001

*The Baby Arrives…
And Changes EVERYTHING*

Dear Everyone,

(Actually, that's not true… "Everyone" isn't getting this letter. Just you and a few other people we know. Sending "Everyone" this letter would be unaffordable - costing roughly $3.64 billion dollars in stamps.)

Our new life with our little angel began at 3:00 AM on Sunday, July 8th. I was lying in bed, minding my own dreams, when my body was jolted. Judging by the way my body was bounced, I knew instantly that either a very pregnant woman had just sat down or our dresser had fallen onto our bed. My eyelids flew open to see my wife grinning at me, "I think I'm in labor."

It was the word "think" that must have shut down my brain, because I rolled over and told her to wake me up when she was *sure*.

She said, "Okay," and left the room.

Within 6.5 nanoseconds, the words "I'm in" and "labor" truly registered. I threw off the covers and nearly flipped the mattress, as I hurled myself into the living room. My wife was circling the room, reading the classic *Labor for Dummies*.

I asked, "Did you say you were *in labor*?!"

"I think so," she said calmly - still scanning her book.

"How long have you been up?" I asked.

"Four hours."

"*Four hours*?! Why didn't you wake me up *earlier*?"

"I was afraid it might just be gas from the Mexican food we ate for dinner."

Hmmmm.

Like a pit crew, we raced into action. My wife hustled (wobbled gingerly) into the shower to shave her legs. Apparently in a new study by world renowned OB-GYN, Dr. Total Wasteoftime, clean shaven legs are the first crucial step to successful baby delivery. Meanwhile - I packed the car like a madman - loading up our suitcase, pillows, and a Weber grill.

We sped to the hospital and hustled to check-in. (The gum-drop shaped nurse at the check-in desk didn't seem to share our belief that check- in should happen in an up-tempo fashion.)

Besides that, I observed a few more important facts:

1. Too many questions by check-in nurse directed at woman in labor = Bad
2. Epidural = Good

The whole process was a whirlwind.

The doctor glided in and asked, "Okay Dad, wanna' come down here with me and witness the birth of your first child?"

I declined - citing my preference to stay "upstream."

Five pushes later, our lives changed for the better - forever.

I kissed Rana's forehead and stared at this beautiful (albeit slimy) baby being passed around the room of nurses in almost perfect choreography. Everything seemed to be moving in slow motion - until something unexpected happened: Our son peed on the nurse. I'm not sure what it was - maybe similar to the inner pride a father feels when his son lets loose his first burp - but I puffed up a bit. The yellow-stained nurse smiled politely, and continued doing her job, as if she wasn't surprised by the incident. (Side note: I don't ever want a job where being peed on becomes an expectation from my place of employment.)

*If you're wondering about Daddy cutting the umbilical cord, I didn't. During our labor classes, the presenter made the mistake of saying the following: "Now the cord doesn't cut very easily - you have to really work and saw at it..." *Work and saw*, huh? I'm out, thanks.

FIRST HOUR ALONE WITH BABY

I'll tell you – generally – privacy is nice. After being exposed to every person employed at the hospital – I think the hair-netted, cafeteria lunch lady and the head of maintenance checked on us at one point - eventually they *all* trickled away. When that last nurse left and the door closed, you'd think you'd be relieved. But, this may have been the scariest moment in my life.

You mean we have to take care of this thing all by ourselves????

DADDY'S FIRST DIAPER CHANGE:

All eyes on Daddy. Baby screaming. Daddy peels back the tabs. Daddy is frightened and only breathes through his mouth. The baby doll Daddy practiced on didn't squirm like this - or smell like this…Daddy has never seen this color (or consistency) before. Mommy hands Daddy a baby wipe. Daddy grabs baby's feet and begins to wipe everything. Baby doesn't like it. Baby is kicking daddy. Daddy fumbles with a new diaper. Everyone in the room seems to be timing Daddy. Daddy can't seem to work the tabs. The tabs are stuck to Daddy's shirt. Now the tabs are stuck to baby. Now the tabs are stuck to the diaper. Now the diaper is too loose - and backwards. Daddy doesn't care. Daddy hands the saggy diapered baby to Mommy. Mommy is proud of Daddy.

HOSPITAL SLEEPING ARRANGEMENTS FOR DAD

Unless you're currently employed as an Acrobat of China, you're not sleeping in that chair they call a "recliner."

RUNNING LATE AND ARRIVING HOME

I always thought the worst drivers I'd ever seen were the residents of San Francisco (and my own wife). Now I can admit my mistake. The worst drivers in the world are actually circling hospitals like buzzards - waiting for new, freaked-out parents and their newborns, to pull out of the parking lot.

I've now discovered why new parents and their small children are always running late. The length of our car-ride? Tripled. I employed an overly-cautious extended-pause at every stop sign. I also drove significantly *below* the speed limit, choking the steering wheel as I repeatedly whipped my head toward the back seat to make sure Canton was still breathing.

As we finally pulled into our driveway, my heart was pounding. It was a crazy mix of excitement and fear – like standing at the front of the line just before a roller coaster arrives to whisk you away. And the moment you wobble through the front door with the car seat carrier, the roller coaster begins…You think you're ready. But the ride has surprises you could never have imagined…

A comedian once joked that all babies must be secret agents, because the minute they're born they try to "break you" with sleep deprivation. The joke isn't funny because it is true. Our first night at home with the baby could be summed up like this: Baby crying. Mommy crying. Daddy crying. No one sleeping. Dog glad he was neutered.

The major mistake we made was purchasing a baby monitor. The baby monitor was a mistake because the point of the monitor was that it was supposed to give us peace of mind by allowing us to hear Canton if he started crying. Let me be real clear: parents don't *need* a monitor to STATICALLY ECHO the sound of their baby crying. When your baby cries, you can hear it juuuuussstttt fine. In addition, the monitor picked up *every* other sound coming from our baby's room – gurgles, sniffles, snorts, thumps, doinks, bumps, grunts, wheezes, kicks, and chortles…All of these sounds bore a strikingly resemblance to a possible burglar rummaging through our home. Thus, the use of a baby monitor meant only one thing: we were *not* going to be sleeping.

Sleep deprivation is no laughing matter – especially by night #8... But luckily, there is a warning sign: inability to create a coherent sentence. It's really alarming when it happens - like the body has suddenly realized it has gone too long without sleep.

A quote uttered by my wife: "We slept with the breastfed pillow resting because my eyes were snoring."

My slurred response: "Your breasts can change your own diapers."

Smart-alecks say the lack of sleep isn't all that bad. It's how you feel the next day. Okay, that's a little like the person that says the fall out of a 100 story building doesn't kill you... it's the landing. Well, sleep deprivation is "the landing" all day long. Thankfully, we adapted to the new lack-o-sleep patterns (C-O-F-F-E-E and the Home Shopping Network), and began to truly enjoy our baby...

And through the tears and possible moments of clinical insanity that come from not sleeping, when your baby finally drifts to sleep on your shoulder and all that surrounds you is the sweet smell of their head and the soft whisper of their breathing, all the years of life you felt had been sucked from your body are peacefully injected back in...

And it must be that peaceful injection stuff that energizes parents into their daily superhero roles. I witnessed this recently while observing Rana breastfeeding, painting her toenails, playing "fetch" with the dog, and ordering a pizza over the phone (at the same time). I was impressed and knew I must improve my parental multitasking...And just so you know, at the printing of this letter, I'm proud to announce that I am currently able to heat a bottle AND hold my son at the same time. Soon, I plan to add "watch televised sports" to coincide with the other two. Baby steps, you know?

I also want it known that I have been working on my ability to be a helpful contributor when we take our son out in public.

Example: The baby "breaks the seal" of the diaper at the mall. Simple solution, right?

Rana: "Did you bring a diaper bag, honey?"

Daddy: "Uh. Uh. Did *you* bring a diaper bag?"

Rana: "No, I brought the baby and these uncomfortably, oversized breasts to feed the baby."

Daddy: "Oh....Well, let me see if we can borrow some napkins and a roll of tape from that pretzel kiosk over there."

Rana: "Good idea, MacGyver."

TIME TO TIE THIS THING UP...

Rana and I asked our friend, Becky, to paint Canton's nursery. (And, I'm so glad we chose pale yellow for the paint color because on several occasions Daddy wasn't quite fast enough in stopping Canton's surprisingly high-powered pee fountain from reaching the wall near the changing table.)

Anyway, besides the walls, Becky transformed Canton's ceiling into a gorgeous fading blue sky with fluffy, white clouds. I added blue wallpaper stars to the walls as well. Becky thought something might still be missing, so she told me to write a poem for her to paint around the tops of all four walls. This is what I came up with:

SWEET ANGEL OF OURS,

THE SKY YOU SEE,

IS FULL OF ENDLESS,

POSSIBILITIES

At the time, it was a poem for the future of our son. But since September 11th, it's taken on a new meaning ...In a sense, it's a poem for all of us. The terror and smoke-filled sky we see is ours.

But we choose whether to immerse ourselves in doubt or hope. We choose to love or to hate.

Rana and I look at the sky we see: all of you. We can't help but be thankful not only that we have you as friends - but that the world has you. The world is going to come out of this mess because of people like you. And, hopefully, because of children like Canton.

May God bless you this holiday season and fill your hearts with hope and peace.

Love,

John, Rana, Baby Canton, and Montana the Wonderpup

CHAPTER SIX
Christmas 2002

*Baby Milestones, Gymnastics
& First Baby Party Fiasco*

S

eason's Greetings,

(Okay - I'm off to a great start here. I try for a new heading each and every year. But this one is odd. Think about it. When was the last time December wished you a happy holiday - or even had the common decency to drop you a line? Never. Exactly. Just to make sure we're clear: it isn't the season greeting you, but us - The Post Family.)

The Post Family has been inundated with milestones this year. So have a seat, the next milestone may be longest Christmas letter of all time...

Sadly, for some first-time parents, it's hard for them to enjoy their infant's milestones because they're so busy being lunatics. (The parents are the lunatics – not the infants... though the infants can sometimes act like crazyheads too...) Anyway, parents encourage their babies to accomplish certain actions with a fervor that I can only liken to those "energetic" folks who clap their hands and stomp their feet at a frog jumping contest - trying to make their frog get to the finish line first. (No need to remind you we live in Missouri.)

At some point, when Canton was still drooling, Rana casually suggested we sign him up for a sport. Yep, you heard that right. My wife suggested it. I was all in.

"He's a little small to start pee-wee football," I said.

"Not *that* sport," she said. "I was thinking of getting him into gymnastics."

"I thought you said a 'sport?'" I asked.

"Gymnastics *is* a sport," she said.

But I was hesitant. Rana reassured me that it wasn't so much for actual "gymnastics," but that it would be great to quote, "develop coordination and further his gross motor development." I think all that textbook talk was meant to confuse me (and it did), but I wasn't going to be thrown off my main concern.

"Is he gonna' have to wear a leotard?" I asked.

"You're dumb." I believe those were her exact words.

So I agreed. Canton would take gymnastics classes, called Tiny Tumbling Tots, with Rana's old gymnastics coach, Borishki.

I remember flopping into the car after Canton's first "practice." I told Rana she must be mistaken. The real name of the class should be: "Daddy, Was That Popping Sound Your Hamstring?" I got the most extensive workout of anyone there - crawling and chasing Canton around the gym through obstacle courses that a trained lab-rat would have a tough time navigating. But, I'm getting more flexible as each week passes.

The class began with all the critters and their parents sitting down on a circle of carpet squares. Borishki then played a fun children's song, and we all did an organized activity like the "Hokey Pokey" or "Wheels on the Bus." During the first class, Canton's favorite activity was called, "I'll Do Whatever I Damn Well Please." He mastered it immediately, but then slowly began to be interested in joining his fellow Tumbling Tots as they Hokied and Pokied on the Bus.

To the casual observer - it was probably quite funny. A class full of chubby ankle-biters who could barely talk, but whose camcorder-toting parents were trying to prove to the world that their child was the most athletic one-year-old alive.

Dad #1: "Look at little Dawson jump up and down on the trampoline." (Sir, you were yanking up and down on his arms.)

Mommy #2: "Little Timberland can do a perfect somersault!" (Ma'am, you just whipped the child's feet out from under her.)

And then there was my wife.

Rana: "Canton is the cutest one here." (Okay – she was correct.)

All joking aside, the class was great. Canton's only 17 months old – but his coordination (and mine) is really improving. Recently, Borishki suggested we enroll Canton in Tiny Tot Aquatics.

Splash, splash, glub, glub. We'll see…

BABY'S FIRST WORD

Parenthood is full of momentous "firsts." But sometimes, once the "firsts" have happened, you realize they've become "forevers." For example, parents beg for their child's first word. They make stupid sounds, faces, and gestures to try to encourage their child to talk. And then it happens. They say it. Whether it's "Mama," "Dada," or "No." Once it's uttered, there is no going back. They will never - no matter how much you may wish they would - stop talking.

We were dying to hear Canton's first word. With as much as Rana talked to him, there was no telling what it might be. I was hoping for "Daddyisreallyawesome." But I liked Rana's Dad, George's strategy. At the daycare, he had been saying the random word, "light" to Canton throughout the day. That way, when Canton blurted that word out eventually, we'd know it was all because of Grandpa George…

While we waited for that elusive first word, I think all first-time parents have asked themselves this question: "Was that an *actual* word my child just said?" What sounds like "gouulabahlaaagchewwwwzzzzzz" can be translated by most first-time parents as, "I laugh at Gouda cheese." Thus, the wicked game of phonetic analysis began…

I was home alone this Spring with the little fella' when he looked at me and said, "Dada."

"What did you say?" I asked.

He just looked at me. Since I was positive it was my title, and not a bout of gas, I made my emergency-first-word-alert-phone call to Rana.

"He said, 'Dada!'" I gleamed.

"He *did?*" she said. (This reminded me of the identical tone I once heard from my own parents when, as a youth, I tried to convince them that my teddy bear had eaten one of my M&Ms.)

"I'm serious!" I insisted.

"That's greaaaaaaat," she said. I heard her scribbling - probably the number for the hearing aide store down the street.

"Well, this *Dada* hopes you have a great day," I said and hung up.

The next day at Grandma's daycare, Canton said, "Dada" to Grandma. I'm not particular. He can point to a bag of dog food and say "Dada" for all I care. I am content in the fact that it was his first word.

I'm sure "Momma" (his 5th word - after "Dada," "ball," "book," and "puppy") will come to grips with it someday.

CANTON'S FIRST B-DAY PARTY

It's a well- known fact that my wife can't cook. Well, she can't bake... or prepare... or broil... or grill... or wok... or sauté... or flambé very well either. (Check that: She flambés *exceptionally* well.)

74

Rana once substituted Cajun Creole seasoning powder for cinnamon because, (and I quote) "It looked the same to me." So when she told me she was going to be baking for Canton's first birthday party, I was ~~intrigued~~ frightened.

She was so proud of herself: "We're going to have Rainbow Fish decorations, you know, like the children's book. And, we're going to have a cake in the shape of a fish!"

"Wal-Mart sells a fish-shaped cake?" I joked.

"*I'm* going to make it," she said surely.

I smiled. I laughed. I fell on the floor.

"Jessica's going to help me," she said. (I was relieved, since our dear friend Jessica had once made me iced Halloween cookies in the shape of little Frankenstein heads and they were delicious.) It was set. Team RanaJessica would begin the baking process at 5:00 p.m. the evening before his party... At 11:30 p.m. that night, I peeked into our kitchen. It was horrifying.

A cartoon fish autopsy was taking place. Flour dusted the floor, and blue icing was *everywhere*. Toothpicks (like a mowed down mini-forest) littered the counters. The girls were drowning in blue sugar sprinkles and sweet-tart fish scales. Apparently, they didn't notice the destruction around them. Their only concern seemed to be Mr. Rainbow Fish's rather large tail that kept crumbling apart – in spite of the toothpicks.

Soon, extra pieces of cake were being surgically melded together. Fins became make-shift tails. Fish parts were becoming interchangeable. Scary. Our dog, Montana, who is gleefully ever-present when food is nearby, trembled by the back door, anxious to escape.

Rana, usually calm and cool, looked at the clock. She was beginning to lose it. I asked if I could help.

75

"Yes, please let the dog out," she said, pointing to the door.

I opened the door and whispered to the dog, "Be free."

As Montana dashed outside, I noticed a plump, green object leap between my legs and dart under the refrigerator.

"FROG!" Rana screamed.

I joked, "It's a little late to be changing the party's theme."

She glared at me, and Jessica gave me the "Poor Choice" head shake. Rana then started complaining that I had slow reflexes. (If she had signed Canton and me up for those gymnastics classes earlier, we wouldn't have that problem, would we?)

"WE will NOT have a FROG hopping around the KITCHEN during the PARTY tomorrow," she said emphatically.

"Okay," I muttered and proceeded to pull the fridge forward. No frog.

"Where is it?!"

"I don't know," I shrugged. I kept pushing and tugging the fridge and kept seeing no frog.

I imagined this frog acting like a soldier - crawling commando style on its belly and looking up, so he could stay directly under the fridge wherever I moved it. That thought made me laugh. Rana wasn't laughing. After twenty minutes, I finally got the froggy out with the help of a spatula- but not before it (the frog, not the spatula) peed from terror on the kitchen floor.

The girls finished the cake around midnight, covered it with a tepee of aluminum foil, and stuck it in the fridge. The rule was that no one was allowed to open the fridge to see if the tail had fallen off again until an hour before the party. (Out of sight, out of mind, I guess?)

The next morning my milk less Cheerios tasted yummy.

When the fridge door was finally opened, the tail stood tall.

The party was a hit. We had friends and family over, and my mom caught a last second plane from D.C. to surprise us. (The other surprise was that no one was hospitalized from eating Rana's fish cake… Probably because of Jessica.)

And most importantly, our marriage (and the fish tail) had stayed intact.

HALLOWEEN

I might mention that Canton dressed up as a giraffe for Halloween. Adorable? Yes. A little short? Perhaps.

HOLIDAY AIR-TRAVEL WITH A BABY

Don't.

TIME TO END

I heard a quote on a TV show the other night about the lives of teachers and their students in a rough downtown school. A veteran teacher was passing a brand new teacher in the parking lot after school. The new teacher had had quite a tough day. She looked at the older teacher and asked, "Does it get any easier?"

He smiled and said, "Not if you're doing it right."

I thought it was an awesome quote – kind of a Carpe Diem ("Seize the Day") type of thing.

So as this upcoming year brings its mixture of blessings and challenges, I pray that at the end of each day, we can all say that we "did it right."

Thank you for all you do for us. We are so fortunate to call you our family and friends.

Love,

Dada, Rana,
Canton, and Montana

CHAPTER SEVEN
Christmas 2003

The Terrible Twos

Holiday greetings from Missouri, the "Land Flowing with Milk and Cows",

As far as I could tell, things with The Post Family had been so "normal" this year, that I contemplated ditching this letter - and just sending a card. But my friend, Bobo told me, "You *have* to send the letter, it's my favorite bathroom reading material." Oh, well in that case…

But what should I write? You don't want to hear about Uncle Harry's hemorrhoid surgery or Aunt Roberta's latest run-in with local law enforcement. (Now you literal people are scanning your memory banks searching for Itchy Uncle Harry and Outlaw Aunt Roberta. They were used for emphasis and don't actually exist. Or, at least I don't think they do - wouldn't that be embarrassing?!)

Anyway, I was at a loss. But, after an hour of sitting in front of the flashing cursor on the computer monitor and fearing my left butt cheek might be permanently asleep, I dragged myself to Rana.

"There's nothing to write about," I whined.

She nodded and then grinned, "I have a few words that might help jumpstart the process: 'Terrible Twos.'"

Writer's Block Be Gone!

TWO is a magical (by "magical," I mean "hellish") age, when the word "**NO**" is fired around by toddlers like bullets on a battlefield. This battlefield is familiar to most parents since they find themselves entrenched there approximately 105 times a day. Some notable Canton skirmishes include the "It-Doesn't-Look-Like-Elmo-So-I'm-Not-Eating-It" Crisis, to the "I'll-Launch-A-Pee-Fountain-Out-Of-The-Bathtub" Discrepancy. Some battles are won by parents in mere minutes through the use of solitary confinement (Time Out), while other battles take a little more patience to win. Occasionally, the family dog becomes a target, as was the case in the "I-Will-Ride-Him-Because-He-Looks-Like-A-Pony" Catastrophe.

(Montana won that one without mommy or daddy having to get involved – but Canton was left with a golf-ball sized lump on his head as a parting gift.)

TWO is also a special time, because the child's vocabulary has expanded from 2 or 3 words to 2.3 million words. I remember how anxiously we awaited Canton's first word. Now, we wonder if he can be silent for 4 consecutive seconds.

Sometimes, the words he utters are very easy to understand. Ex: "I no like it!" Other times we have no idea what he's saying - but he does. And he acts like we are dysfunctional idiots because we can't understand the words he's saying so clearly.

He'll say something like, "I want Guuuddfaa." - which clearly doesn't make sense.

I'll repeat, "You want Guuuddfaa?" (Notice all the letters are spoken in the exact same sequence.).

He'll say more loudly, "No! Dada, *Guuuddfaa!*"

Huh?

If a word that Canton loves (or hates) is spoken in the next state, he can hear it. So, we've had to stay one step ahead of him in some cases by spelling words out as our special secret code. She'll say, "I think S-O-M-E-O-N-E needs a N-A-P." The code can also be beneficial when using words we don't want Canton to learn. "C-R-A-P" currently works well when Daddy's watching sports. It's wonderful!

(Tiny problem that's developed here: we've started unconsciously using our code with other adults. I'll call my friend, "You wanna go shoot P-O-O-L and grab some D-I-N-N-E-R?" You wouldn't believe how this incapacitates a perfectly intelligent grown up.)

With the frustration that sometimes accompanies Canton's budding independence/vocabulary, there *are* times when he says things that - well - just make you smile...

I must start out with what might be the most beautiful words Canton has spoken to date. Side note: The addition of a child to the family means several major changes in the household. Among other things, Daddy's collection of movies like "Die Hard" and "Gone in 60 Seconds" have been suffocated by an uncountable number of Sesame Street videos. (I think those things must R-E-P-R-O-D-U-C-E at night, when we're not looking.) Anyway, it was Sunday and Canton and I were flopped on the couch watching the conclusion of the video classic, "Elmo Drives Daddy to the Insane Asylum." Canton patted my leg - which I assumed meant that he wanted me to replay the video.

Instead he smiled and said, "Dada?"

I said, "Yeah, bud?"

"Dada...I wanna' watch football now."

(Insert angelic choir music here...)

A FEW OTHER MEMORABLE QUOTES

*We were driving in the car and Rana was playing entertainer in the back seat with Canton. Canton poked Rana in the boob and said, "I want that ball." Rana was mouth-open, mortified.

Canton poked her boob again and repeated, "I want that ball, Mommy."

I laughed so hard, I nearly drove the car into a cow pasture. But, Rana was very alarmed - her Child Life background didn't prepare her for this. She asked me, "What do I *say?*"

I said, "Tell him he can't play with it - it's Daddy's."

She jokingly smacked me in the back of the head, I yelled, "Ouch," and Canton burst into hysterical laughter.

Perfect distraction tactic, Mommy... That "Smack, Ouch, Laugh" game was played all the way home.

*I accidentally passed gas (loudly) in the kitchen. Canton from his high chair chuckled, "Haha. Dada pooped."

*We were at the zoo. We had been preparing Canton to see his favorite animal - the elephant. We finally got to the "arena," and he saw the tusked giant towering above us. Canton gasped, and immediately tried to climb the fence while yelling, "I hold it!"

THE GREAT CHRISTMAS PICTURE FIASCO OF 2003

Segue: You know how all great paintings/pictures have titles: "Mona Lisa," "The Last Supper," and "Marilyn Monroe's Skirt is Blown up on the Sewer Grate?" We decided that if Canton were naming our first official family picture, he'd call it "Watch Me Punt My Parents."

Mike, my roommate from college, agreed to take our Christmas picture this year. He obviously was oblivious to what he was getting himself into. We went to a charming section of St. Louis called Old St. Charles for the Christmas ambience. The setting, weather, and lighting were all perfect. The only problem was that Canton was possessed by evil spirits just as our friend readied the camera - and I had left the Holy Water at home.

I must say that this is one of the funny (not really) things I've noticed about parenthood. At a supermarket, you can witness a two-year-old tot poking asparagus at the live lobster tank while the parent says loudly, "I don't understand! He *never* acts this way." I used to laugh at what I presumed was an awful lie. Now I know, that it was obviously not a lie. The child had apparently *never* violated the lobster before - it *was* a first time thing - and the parents were powerless to anticipate it... Likewise, I was unprepared to handle Canton trying to kick my wife during our photo shoot. If we had been thinking clearly, we could have just changed the whole picture theme to the three of us imitating the high-kicking NYC Rockettes. But, instead I found myself saying, "I don't know what's gotten into him. He *never* acts like this." Mike smiled patiently (he has two children of his own) and attempted to make sounds like Donald Duck to get Canton to look at the camera. At that point, I think I heard Canton mumble in a possessed voice, "You think a lame duck noise is going to get me to look at you, fool?"

I turned to Mike and joked, "If you could pull E-L-M-O out of your B-U-T-T, he *might* look." Mike appeared confused.

For a change of pace, I began heaving Canton into the air over my head. A few cute shots of air born Canton laughing hysterically show my face deeply contemplating, "Drop, or catch, drop or catch?"

The majority of the pictures show us holding Canton in a headlock to get him to be still. One move Rana used might be implemented by the USA Greco Roman Wrestling Team in the upcoming Olympics...We were very proud.

POTTY TRAINING

Not there yet. Still waiting for Disney to come out with a video titled, "Winnie the Pooh, Really Does Go Pooh - and Other Potty Training Tricks."

WHAT'S SANTA BRINGING

"Santa," apparently being inconsiderate and deaf, has purchased Canton his very own drum set. It lights up, has a real bass pedal, and even a head-set. While I'm sure "Our Little Drummer Boy" will be thrilled, I hope Mrs. Claus grants my only wish this year: noise cancelling headphones.

FOOTBALL

This year, I "inherited" the 7th grade team from the year before that had only won a single game. No one had any expectations - including me. Rana warned me, "Don't even think about promising this bunch that you'll shave your head again if they win four games." (I agreed because I figured that shaved legs weren't the same thing - kidding, just kidding...)

In our first game, my wife was fairly confident I would not be shaving anything after watching the following event unfold on the field: On the very first play, the opposing quarterback fumbled and the ball bounced far away from everyone - except for one of my players. We'll call him "Duh." As the quarterback from the other team scrambled on his hands and knees to recover the ball he'd fumbled, "Duh" approached the ball slowly. As he bent over it with his hands on his hips, he alternated between looking at the ball at his feet and watching the opposing quarterback crawling toward the ball. I, along with the sell-out crowd of 140, was screaming at "Duh" to fall on the ball. Apparently, our utterances mattered little as he watched the other player recover his own fumble. As "Duh" headed toward me, I met him halfway out on the field. I said (yelled), "Why didn't you fall on the ball?!!!!" He looked at me - dead serious - and said, "I'm not sure, coach. I just thought that kid was up to something *tricky*." Good grief.

In spite of several similar bone-headed plays, we somehow managed to finish the season 4-1-1. The parents and players were thrilled. My dad even flew out to surprise me for the last game: a 30-6 win over our arch-rival school. I mentioned all this because I recently turned in my football coaching resignation so I can start spending more time with my family. While I'm a little sad (not about spending more time with my family, but about my football coaching career being over), I'll be forever sustained by some amazing memories.

TIME TO END

Rana and I were flying around the house last week wrapping presents, attempting to strap felt reindeer antlers to Montana, and trying to figure out which of the 4561 light bulbs was loose causing three strands of lights to flicker annoyingly. Anyway, Rana and I were really in the zone. Canton was wide-eyed, tugging at us and really taking personal ownership of this Christmas by saying things like, "My Cwistmas twee!" and "My blinky lights!" (Oh, if only we *wanted* them blinking!)

Anyway, I'm pretty sure we were being a bit too dismissive of our son by saying, "Yeah, yeah, bud. Ok, Mommy and Daddy are busy."

So Canton went over to his little manger play set and said, "My cows." (I guess the Fisher Price people thought Jesus was born in Missouri?)

Then he said, "My baby."

It instantly hit us, and we both looked up and smiled. We were so busy "running around and getting it done," that we were starting to lose sight of the little things that make this season so special: the beautifully decorated tree, the warmth of Christmas music, our precious son, Canton, and THE precious Son, Jesus...

And we'd like to thank *you* for being such a special part of our lives as well - with all the love, support, and prayers you shower on us. We are truly blessed.

May this season and the New Year fill your hearts with joy and peace.

We love you all,

The P-O-S-T-S

CHAPTER EIGHT
Christmas 2004

*Potty Training, Thumb Sucking
& The Independent Threes*

Merry Christmas (an odd phrase if you really think about it since Christmas isn't able to possess the feeling of bubbly joyfulness),

This year, Rana and I contemplated getting in touch with the merriness of Christmas by trudging out into nature and cutting down our own Christmas tree in the woods. I had a romantic vision of my wife and I pulling Canton on a sled through the snowy wilderness, so we could cut down the perfect tree. We ended up being too chicken to do that, mostly because I'm not very good with an axe. Instead, we decided to pick out a tree in the church parking lot.

Our friend Jessica was with us because she's practically family and also to ensure Canton wasn't crushed by a Frasier Fir. We got to the lot early in the day so we were the only ones there. Thus, we were able to get the volunteer Tree Guy's individual attention and "expert opinion."

He was smiling as he walked over to us, but I wanted to tell him to run the opposite way. He didn't know my wife - or know of her world renowned ability to tell if a tree was missing 3 pine needles on the 56th branch. I told him I hoped he hadn't been to the gym that day, because he was about to lift enough trees to skip the gym for the next year. He chuckled - obviously not understanding that I was serious.... As predicted, the poor guy had to hold up 34 trees - sometimes two at a time for comparison's sake - as Rana inspected them one at a time. She shook her head – "Too short," "Too dumpy," "Too misshapen..." The Tree Guy was beginning to look offended, but I promised him that my wife was *only* referring to the trees.

Finally, we were down to two. (The tree guy's arms were beginning to tremble noticeably.)

"Dat one," Canton pointed. It wasn't one of the final two we had selected but it was obvious that Canton had a tender heart, because if there was a tree in the forest that all other trees would

91

have made fun of - it was the one he pointed to. Anyway, Jessica distracted Canton, while Rana and I decided the BIGGEST of the two trees we had selected was the way to go.

The Tree Guy smiled, as he leaned the tree toward me. Then, one of his arms fell off.

With his other hand outstretched, he told me I owed $61.

"Sixty-one dollars!?" I asked in disbelief, as I scribbled out the check. "Are Christmas trees endangered?"

The whole Christmas Tree Deal is a total scam. It's like the way roses suddenly cost 17 bucks per stem on Valentine's Day - then the next day you can go out and buy 100 roses in a vase for $9.99 at the local gas station. Same with Evergreens. Most doctors' prognosis for a cut down Christmas tree in a parking lot would be something like, "I'm sorry. With good hydration, one month - tops." In spite of this, the Evergreen's stock value in December is ludicrous. January through mid-November when they're thriving in the forest - no one cares about the Evergreen... Well, we decided that if we were going to get hosed on the Christmas Tree Deal anyway, we might as well get hosed at the church. At least that way all the money was going to God.

We don't own a truck like the other 98% of Missouri residents, so we had to strap the tree to the roof of our car. It was only when the tree was on top of our car that I noticed how truly big the tree was. Actually, it appeared to be longer than our car. (No - I'm not overcompensating for anything.)

As it turned out, this was the windiest night of the year. The tree was literally thumping up and down on the roof of the car as we pulled out of the parking lot. We could see the tip of the tree dipping over the hood. (I flashed back to 1998, when Rana and I attempted to transport a new mattress with box spring on the roof of our car in a 46 MPH crosswind. I think the Missouri Highway

Patrol made an informational video of the event called, "Flying Mattresses: Swerve or Duck.")

So the tree was thumping against the roof like a bad rap song, while Canton was kicking the back of Rana's seat trying to mimic the beat. I was driving as *slowly* as possible to avoid launching our tree and to avoid decapitating several night joggers who were passing us on the left.

Rana patted my leg and grinned, "Now, *this* would be great material for the Christmas letter."

The next evening, Rana and I sat down to decide what else in our hectic year we wanted to write about. Rana presented at a Child Life conference held at the Mayo Clinic, I just got an "A" in my first class heading toward my Master's Degree in educational administration, and we've traveled some. Rana had her wallet stolen while at church. (We wondered if our arch nemesis No-Pay Charlene had been granted an early release for good behavior.) But, as we continued to review the past year, we kept getting interrupted:

Canton: "Mommy, Montana licked my head!"

Canton: "Daddy, the Cwristmas twee attacked me!"

Thus we realized, the focus of this last year has really been on the innumerable needs and concerns of our 3-year-old, Canton.

This year has been a whirlwind. Tornado. Gale. Hurricane. Cyclone. That comes with parenthood. It's in the brochure in fine print. Somewhere after, "…and they'll actually wipe their nose on your arm…" but before, "…they will leave a 'floating surprise' in the bathtub…"

Truthfully, I think parenthood is the best thing that's ever happened to us. But it makes us recall the days when we had no kids. What in the world did we do with our time? Did we

93

accomplish *anything*? I think we may have been the two most unproductive people on planet earth. I remember us thinking we were busy back then. We could barely eat dinner and watch TV at the same time. And if the phone rang? It was all over.

Parenthood forces you into productivity: You must learn to search for the missing pieces of a giraffe puzzle, while Mommy tries to squeeze in a 30 second shower. You must be able to wrestle with your child on the bed (to distract the child so Mommy can finish drying off from the shower in peace), catch the last 2 minutes of ESPN (because sports are important), while turning hot dogs on the grill (because hot dogs are about the only thing your child will eat besides yogurt). You have to then be able to call the doctor (when your son breaks three of your ribs after jumping onto your chest), order a pizza (since the hot dogs now look like burnt sticks), plus put socks on your scampering child - who just happens to have the three missing giraffe puzzle pieces clenched between his toes. Parents are an incredible species!

But parents are at their finest when they patiently try to engage in conversations with their toddlers. These conversations – if you can call them conversations – wither the most articulate mature adult:

Toddler: "Is Elmo green?"

Adult: "No, honey, Elmo's red."

Toddler: "No, he's not."

Adult: "Yes, bud, Elmo IS red. He's not green."

Toddler: "Maybe he's blue."

Adult: "No. Look, he's red. R-E-D, red. Not green, not blue; not polka dot, he's red - like a tomato."

Toddler: "Tomatoes aren't red."

Adult (?): "Yes-huh they are!!!!!!"

But besides conversing with your kid, there are other issues that come up that the parenting brochure never prepared you for. But I wasn't worried. Since Rana has had so much child development background, I leave a lot of parental decisions to her. She tells me what we're going to do, and I don't ever have any better ideas, so I follow along... Until the thumb sucking ordeal. Canton would suck his thumb to drift off to sleep - no problem. Canton would suck his thumb while doing everything else – including eating. Potential problem.

"What are we gonna' do?" I asked. "His thumb sucking is out of control."

"I have an idea," Rana said. "I think we should ask him to give us his thumb."

"What!?" I asked with my eyes bugging out.

Rana was serious. "When he's not sleeping, we're going to ask him to give us his thumb. We'll tell him he can have it back at sleep times."

I stared at her for about 10 seconds. Then I laughed so hard and long, that I almost choked. When I regained my composure, I said, "That'll NEVER work."

The next morning Rana sat down on Canton's bed and said, "Okay, you're going to give Mommy your thumb."

Canton looked at her funny and held out his thumb. Rana tugged gently on it, stuck "it" in her pocket, and said, "Thank you. You can have it back when you sleep."

Unbelievable. It worked like a charm. To this day - he asks us to give him his thumb before he sleeps. And when he wakes up, he sticks out his thumb like a hitchhiker and actually insists that we take it away.

Score one - or 1,000,000 for those counting at home - for Rana. But while the thumb-sucking deal could be cured with a single good idea, potty training proved to be a much different story...

If I were to describe this year in terms of one word, it would be "Pooh." (I'm not talking about "Winnie the," either.) The "Pooh" I'm referring to is also known as doo-doo, caca, and nasty. Most of our year, you see, has been dedicated to potty training. To dedicate yourself to anything – requires discipline. But when you are dedicating yourself to someone else's bowel movements, it's easy to get discouraged. I told Rana that part of this letter was going to be about our potty training experience. She said, "Oh, that'll be funny." Wrong! There is nothing funny about poop. In case you don't believe me, when was the last time you heard laughter coming out of a bathroom stall?

The peeing part of potty training came easily. Actually, that's not entirely true. At first Canton wouldn't go anywhere - except in his pants. Then Daddy had an idea. (You read that right - "*Daddy!*") I was helping out a friend at his fireworks tent this summer. Canton visited me early one morning. Canton was bouncing up and down and tugging at his pants. I asked him if he had to pee.

He said, "I do!"

I stared at the giant, blue Porta Potty positioned on the side of the tent. (Some companies called them "Porta John" but I find that term highly offensive.) Honestly, I just didn't want Canton to use it. I was afraid he might fall in if I tried to sit him down. Plus, the inside of those things are claustrophobic and stinking scary. Side note: with the over-saturation of clichés in horror movies these days, I wonder why no one has come up with the idea of a Possessed

96

Porta Potty? Now *that* would be terrifying... Anyway, since no one was around, I had an idea.

"Canton, we're going to pee on the grass behind the tent," I proclaimed.

"Pee on da gwass, Dada?"

"Yes, son, pee on da gwass," I repeated.

I helped him behind the tent, and he started to cry. I think he thought he might injure da gwass somehow. After a few minutes, nature called (pardon the pun). He giggled for a few minutes afterward, and he insisted we call Mommy at work to tell her what he had done. I'm not sure Rana was nearly as proud as he (or I) was. From then on, he'd pee anywhere - outside or in a toilet.

The pooping part was a bigger challenge.

Usually we'd get him on the toilet, and he'd scream, "Nooooo!!!!" Occasionally, he'd scream "No!!!!" with such gusto, the "pooh" would accidentally fall out. At that point, Canton would peer into the toilet. He'd still be crying, but laughing excitedly at the same time. But, it was all hit and miss. Nothing consistent.

We tried the parent trap of candy reward: M & M's for going poop in the toilet. (I'm pretty sure this is a major reason the makers of M&Ms are millionaires.) Again, hit and miss.

Grandma's daycare also took an interest in Canton's pooh performance and tried to implement Operation M&M: I came to pick Canton up one day. There were no kids in the living room - just Grandpa George smiling from his recliner. I looked into the bathroom to find 5 little people jumping up and down and cheering around the toilet. I felt like a National Geographic Explorer coming upon an ancient (and secret) tribal ritual. One of the natives - I mean kids - saw me and yelled, "Do you want an M&M?"

"What for?" I asked.

"Canton pooped in the potty!" the boy shouted.

Each child wanted to inspect the first poop in the toilet because they shared in the spoils. "The Pooper" and each child who cheered around the toilet got an M&M. Even Grandpa George got one – because he was being so encouraging from his recliner.

Then one day, when we were at our wits end, Canton came up to me and said, "I don't have to go poop right now." We began to realize that every day with a toddler is "Opposite Day." ("I'm not tired," and "That smell isn't from me" are a few other examples.) He began walking into the bathroom, because "he *didn't* have to go." Makes sense, huh?

As we look back at the wasted hours of conversation about potty training, I recall my Grandma telling us that all parent's concerns about their child's slow walking, talking, thumb sucking, and potty training are a waste: "I never met a normal adult yet, who's still crawling on the floor, sucking his thumb, not talking, and wetting his pants. They'll do what they do, when they do it." Good point.

A FEW CANTON QUOTES

After the potty training was "complete," Canton had a rule that we had to come and inspect anything he "deposited" in the toilet… (What a fun game.)

One day Canton had just finished his business and asked me to inspect. I did. But he insisted Mommy also authenticate the deed.

Mommy did not want to look, but came into the bathroom anyway.

Canton said, "Look, Mommy!" and pointed into the toilet.

Rana clapped her hands and cheered, "Hot dog!"

Canton got a confused look on his face and said, "Mommy, that's not a hot dog. It's poop."

*Canton and I were driving to Grandma's. We passed a pasture full of many cows.

Canton said, "Hey dada, look at da cows!"

"I see them," I replied. And trying to be extra-interactive, I followed-up with, "What are those cows doing?"

Canton giggled, "They eating da gwass."

I said, "Eating grass? Yuck!"

Canton furrowed his eyebrows and shook his finger at me and said, "Hey, dey' like to eat it - just leave dem' alone."

*Canton had been expressing his displeasure when his little buddy Mason got picked up from Grandma's daycare before he did. When the little boy's parents would arrive, Canton would begin acting like - well, a brat. After a few days of this behavior, Grandma pulled Canton aside.

Sternly she said, "When Mason's parents come to pick up today, you will **not** be bad. You will act like a nice boy."

Canton shook his head at her and said, "Grandma, where in the world do you get all your ideas?"

LET'S TRY AGAIN

For those who don't know, we're going to have another baby… and now that I look at that heading above, I can see why some of you might be confused. "Try" in this case merely means that we were apparently successful in "trying" and now, as a result, we are going to "try" to give parenthood with two kids a "try." (If

99

nothing else, this will give us plenty of new material for upcoming Christmas letters. Please keep us in your prayers...)

I'll end this year's letter by mentioning an activity I did with my 7th graders just before Thanksgiving Break. I told them that even on their worst day, they have it better than millions of other children around the world. So, I asked them to write a bulleted list of what they were thankful for. Anything that came to mind was fine, even if it was "shallow." I got, "I'm thankful for my lizard, girls, rap music, Nintendo, Oreos, Mr. Post (kiss-ups), clothes, boys, make-up, and water." The lists went on and on, but I found a few funny ones to share:

*"I'm thankful for books. I **lurn** with them."*

"I'm thankful for food. Without it, we would be dead and really skinny."

*"I am very thankful I'm smart and not **stuped**."* *(Might have been the same kid from the first one?)*

One boy had a long list: #37 was "the green grass" and #38 was "my girlfriend." I made sure I told the girlfriend about that one.

But #1 on one particular student's list struck me the most: *"I'm thankful for every friend I've ever had."*

One hundred and sixty kids - only one response like it. It made me think. We get so busy - hustling and bustling. Sometimes our lives take center stage and the lives of those most important to us take a back seat. This isn't the way it should be - especially during the holidays. So I guess this is a bit of a thankful reflection on our part. You all do so much to enrich our lives. Thank you for being our friends. We love you.

May your New Year be filled with abundance and peace,

The 3 Posts from Missouri – and soon to be 4

CHAPTER NINE
Christmas 2005

Parenthood: Round 2

Guten Tag (That's German for, "I'm really excited to be communicating with all of you via this Christmas letter),

Time is certainly flying by! I'm sure most of you feel the same. It seems like I just wrote you about my trials and tribulations of learning how to change Canton's diaper. (Check that. When changing someone's diaper, there are *no* tribulations.) And now, four years later, Canton has a little brother named Harper. And I am reminded how little I remember about baby catastrophes. All you have to do is walk past my wife to know the story:

"New perfume?" I sniffed.

"Baby butt ointment," Rana replied.

"Oh."

That's right ladies and gentlemen: It's Parenthood, Round 2. When Harper was born on August 25, Rana was forced to admit that the parents-to-children ratio in our household was now 1½ to 2. (Sadly, the ½ was referring to me.) But I am doing much better this time around. For one, I remember spit-up doesn't stain permanently. Secondly, I am remembering that even if I pull the Velcro tabs to create what I think is the tightest diaper ever secured to a baby, sometimes the diaper is still unable to "hold in" everything... But truthfully, what's not to love about a new baby? They generally smell nice and they're sweet. Plus, Harper has provided us with an abundance of joy. By joy, I mean no sleep.

Along with being reminded of that nauseous-no-sleep feeling, we've also rediscovered the joy of milestones. And for fathers, when the milestones have to do with bodily functions, it's that much more exciting – and competitive.

Dad #1: "My boy peed on the changing table when he was five days old."

Dad #2: "Five days? My kid peed on the wall above the changing table at two days old. Is your kid *slow* or just *stupid*?"

103

Upon reading this letter out loud to Rana, Canton scolded me because, according to him, the word "stupid" is a bad word. Canton then remarked that I shouldn't use the word "wiener" either - odd since I didn't say *that* word out loud... Anyway, I want you all to know that my use of the word "stupid" was for emphasis only. I'm not calling anyone "stupid." And for informational purposes - my kid peed on *two* members of the hospital staff *five minutes* after being born.

I suppose I'm kinda' getting ahead of myself, talking about milestones. Because before the milestones can happen, you have to re-prepare yourself (and your home) for the arrival of the baby: Painting pastels in the nursery, baby-proofing EVERYTHING, and baby-preparing EVERYTHING (This included replaying a crying baby tape for the dog, so he didn't freak out. Montana looked at us as if to say, "Yeah, I understood it the first time you did this to me - with the kid over there who's always bossing me around. Come in, get out, sit, shake, roll over... Thanks a lot."). There are prenatal visits, nightly conversations revisiting the possible 31,000 baby names, dusting off high chairs, pulling out baby swings, installing new car seats, and stockpiling diapers. And the constant smell of diaper rash ointment. It's crazy, man! This preparation for a new child sucks away at the fabric of many parents' brains. You're so insanely busy, important items in the calendar seem to take a back-seat to The Due Date.

Here's a pretty good example. ("Good example" does not mean you should imitate me.) Canton got wind that he'd be having a birthday in the summer. He was pretty excited about it. The number four was cool. Gifts/presents were cool, too. Anyway, he began each morning with "Hi, Daddy. Is today my birfday?" On April 3rd, it was pretty cute. By May 10th, I was planning on putting him up for auction on eBay. Mercifully, somewhere around May 20th, he had stopped asking.

Okay - so it was mid-summer and Rana had already left for work. Canton called me from his bed.

"Hi Daddy," he grinned. "Is today finally my birfday?"

Here we go again. "No bud, it's not."

"But today is my birfday. I get pwesents!"

Honestly, I was slightly irritated: "Trust me. It's *not* your birthday."

He dropped his head and did this fake crying thing.

"Cut it out," I said firmly. "It's NOT your birthday. I'll tell you when it's your birthday, okay?"

"Okay," he sighed, and we headed to Grandma's daycare.

I dropped him off, he grudgingly allowed me to kiss his cheek, and I raced off to teach summer school. On the way, my sister, Dawn, called me on my cell phone.

"Hey Bro. Couldn't catch you at home…I'm just calling to wish Canton a happy birthday."

I wrinkled my brow, "Today's not his birthday."

"Today's July 8th," she said. "That *is* his birthday, right?"

Pause.

Now's as good a place as any to mention that Canton is no longer referring to me as "Mister Fibber."

As for what else is going on in Canton's world…The joys of having a preschooler are well documented. One must maintain a level head when your child says, "I call you meanie!" My favorite - which must be a Canton original - "You're not in my club." The first time I heard it, I laughed. Pretty cute. The 43rd time I heard it, I found myself lowering in maturity.

Canton: "You're not in my club, Daddy."

Me: "That's fine."

Canton more loudly: "Did you *hear* me!? You're not in my club!"

Me: "Great! I don't want to be in your stupid club."

Canton: "Oohhh. You said '*stupid*'"

AHHHHHHHHHHH!

Later that day, Canton told me that he wished I'd stop saying "stupid." Ironically, I told him to add that wish to one of his Wish Lists. He has several started.   There's his Christmas Wish List, running concurrently with his Birthday Wish List. (He even had a Potty Training Wish List once upon a time, but it was short with only two items written down.)   In terms of personal value, he holds his Birthday Wish List most dear. Every time he sees something he wants, he asks us to add it to his list.   This list is stuck to the refrigerator door.   Several magnets have perished in the out-of-control expansion of his Birthday Wish List.   It seems the magnets weren't able to support its weight – which is currently 37 pages. Canton says he feels bad about the broken magnets and suggests we add 'buying new magnets' to his list. How thoughtful.

I should also mention that Canton loves to add movie titles to his Wish Lists. His favorites are Baby Einstein and Sesame Street. I actually like those videos because I think they're sort of educational. But the other day, I really paid particular attention to a Sesame Street video we were watching and noticed something kind of alarming: The show takes place on a slummy-looking, inner-city street.   Trash is littered everywhere and the children appear to be running around and riding bikes without any parental supervision whatsoever- in spite of the fact that three of the street's main residents include a 20 foot, non-flying, nuke-yellow bird, an unbathed, unfriendly green monster living in a trash can, and a vampire that likes to count everything he sees. I would have loved to see the faces on the TV executives when the marketing people came to them and said, "Wait until you see what we came up with for our new kids show!" It just goes to show, in this country, anything *really* is possible.

A FEW MORE RANDOM (BUT ASSUMING) CANTON QUOTES

*I was in the kitchen, and Canton smiled at me from the living room. There was something on his front tooth.

I said, "What's on your tooth?"

Canton: "Nothing."

I repeated myself.

Canton: "Nothing, I said!"

I was getting irritated, "I'm not going to ask you again. What's on your tooth?"

Canton turned away and shouted over his shoulder, "It's not a booger!"

(Now, Canton can't be in my club.)

*Canton was pretty jazzed up about Halloween. We told him all week that we were going to the pumpkin patch on the weekend. He was really excited.

Saturday at breakfast, this was me: "Today's going to be a great day, buddy. Remember where we're going?"

Canton shrugged and said, "I don't know."

I said, "Yes you do. Come on. You know where we're going. They're round and orange... We're going to pick_____." I sat there waiting for him to finish the sentence.

107

He thought about it for a few seconds, then his eyes lit up: "We're going to pick *apricots*?!"

*Canton: "I want to name the baby."

Rana: "Uhhhhhhhhhh. What did you have in mind?"

Canton: "Pollywogalina."

Rana: "Oh – we'll just put that one on our No Way List."

*Pre-Harper being born, Canton was dying to meet his baby brother. He desperately wanted to know when Harper was coming. Each day he was becoming more exasperated.

Rana was sitting on the couch.

Canton: "Is Harper coming today?"

Mommy: "No sweetie. Not yet."

Canton rushed up to her and pushed her boob and said, "Will he come if I push this button?!"

*My sister called after Harper was born. Rana was breast-feeding on the couch. Canton got on the phone, and I heard Dawnie ask, "What's Harper doing?"

Canton: "He's drinking Mommy."

It's easy to see that Canton truly loves his new baby bro. Canton talks to Harper constantly and showers his head with daily kisses. (And, apparently that's a wise choice... Our pediatrician told us based on the "charts," Canton better be kind to his little brother, because his "little" brother is going to be *a lot* bigger than him.)

Since we promised ourselves that we'd never turn into those kind of parents that blab on and on about their kids, and now we're five pages into blabbing on and on about our kids, we'll give you a quick update on our lives: We're super. Now, back to our kids...Just kidding.

Rana and I are really enjoying life, cherishing our family time together, and trying to soak in each new milestone, you know? Some dear friends of ours have just experienced one. Their 12 year old daughter successfully drove the car into the garage. The fact that she doesn't have a license and the garage door was closed at the time did not detract from their pride. We have so much to look forward to.

To end, I want to mention that for those of you who aren't aware - Harper's birth didn't go smoothly. His heart rate dropped dangerously low, and Rana was rushed away from me in a swarm of hospital staff for an emergency C-Section. I was stuck in the room by myself - pacing back and forth, praying that Rana and Harper would be okay. It was the longest 25 minutes of my life. But even with my imagination composing the worse possible scenarios, there were moments when I thought about how many people we have in our lives that circle us with their love. That gave me some peace. So, we thank you for being part of "us." Besides Canton and Harper, you all are our most precious gifts from God.

May your holiday and New Year be filled with all you wish for - and more than you ever imagined. We love you!

John, Rana, Canton, Baby Harper, and Montana

CHAPTER TEN
Christmas 2006

Starting School, What's NOT in the Parenting Brochure & Learning to Swim

Holiday Greetings Dear Friends,

We're jumping in this year with exciting news! Canton started preschool. He also got married. Her name is Grace. Canton calls her by her pet name, "Gwace." He told me the tale yesterday afternoon:

Canton: "Daddy, Gwace asked me to marry her!"

Me: "Well, what did you say?"

Canton shrugged: "I said, 'Okay, sure...If you say so.'"

This came as quite a shock to us, since just the day before, Canton had arranged to have Gwace thrown in Time Out for running away from him on the playground. But as the old saying goes, "Time Out heals all wounds." The little couple could not be happier.

Gwace's family is very nice. So is she. In spite of that, we cautioned Canton to sign a Preschool Nup, but he declined. He's a big boy and doesn't need us interfering. Excuse me while I pause writing this letter. Canton can't seem to find his "gween blankey"...Okay, I'm back.

We plan to celebrate his marriage with a sit-down, candle-lit Happy Meal from McDonald's. Rana is pretty emotional. She insists that it isn't just that Canton is growing up too fast. It's also that she's *really* sick of McDonald's food.

So the years seem to be whistling past us. Or maybe that's the sound of Canton and his Best Man, Harper, running circles around us. Any way you slice it, life with two boys, ages one and five, is joyous. And really busy. And very, very loud! Where oh where to begin? Oh, I know! Let us begin with all the stuff that isn't included in The Parenting Brochure.

1. THE CHILDREN'S LAW

Parents are tormented by what normal people refer to as Murphy's Law. The truth is, when you're a parent, Murphy's Law doesn't exist. Instead, you live daily with The Children's Law. Let me give you some of our real-life examples: If a stranger at a restaurant comments that your child is "so well behaved," there is 100% certainty that your child will immediately bite you or fling a fork at the waiter. If a colleague pats your child on the head and remarks how cute they are, your child will instantly sneeze, thus releasing an insanely large, booger-filled, snot-splatter explosion from their right nostril. If you load up the car to take the kids to have their picture taken professionally, your child will slam their own face in the car door. And if you complain to another parent that your child won't ever try anything new to eat, you'll both look out the window to observe your child sniffing and then nibbling on a pinecone. This is the way it goes with kids.

2. HONESTY

It grips five-year-olds like Super Glue. (Speaking of honesty, this might be a good place to mention that you should <u>never</u> substitute Super Glue for regular white glue when playing arts and crafts with your children…) Anyway, kids just HAVE to be honest. Again, let me share with you some real-life examples: In an elevator, they'll point to an obese woman's stomach and ask, "How many babies do you have in there?" You'll snuggle them, when they first wake up, reveling in the sweetness of the moment. Then they will inhale your breath and tell you, "Your air stinks." They'll even shake a church member's hand, then dramatically wipe their hand on their own shirt while demanding, "I need hand sanitizer!"

Their honesty is abundant 24-hours a day. Even at prayer time:

Mommy: "Thank you Lord for our warm beds and our dog Montana."

Me: "Dear Lord, thank you for our family, friends, and wonderful sons, Canton and Harper."

Canton grins: "Dear Lord... Thank you for Mommy's mustache."

Uh, oh.

3. THE INDUSTRIAL REVOLUTION'S CRUELEST JOKE ON PARENTS

The Pez Dispenser. Let me get this straight: You want me to un-wrap that delicate foil without scattering the candy all over the floor? Then, you want me to install the 50 miniscule pieces of candy (2 of which are still stuck in either corner of the foil that never quite ripped), one piece at a time, into the thin slot? The process takes 22 minutes and every ounce of concentration - only to find that your child has inhaled the aforementioned candy in 2.4 seconds and then asks you to load the dispenser again?

4. INDUSTRIAL REVOLUTION'S SECOND CRUELEST JOKE ON PARENTS

The Plexiglas box filled with stuffed animals strategically placed at the entrance of any store where children might enter. (I think the government secretly uses this machine to "break" terrorists.) The craned "claw" has a grip width of a city block. There are 1.2 million stuffed animals lying helplessly beneath the suspended claw. A voice in your head (and the child at your side) convinces you that a blind platypus without arms could pull a stuffed animal out of there... So, surely YOU can! You feel in your pocket, but you don't feel any quarters in there. You remember you spent them all on the Pez Dispenser candy refills. Lucky for you, the store has placed a dollar bill/change machine right next to the claw machine. As you put in the required multiple quarters, you think you hear the machine say, "Idiot." Regardless, you line up the claw. It's hanging directly over the neon colored animal your child wants. Your child is cheering you on. You can't fail. You press the red button. The claw zips down, down, down - right on top of the animal your child wants. The claw makes a motion as if it wants to grip the stuffed plush. Get it, claw! Get it! Nope, the claw can't hear you. Why? Because it's too busy being horribly inefficient and WEAK!

5. TALKING

It doesn't stop. Unless they're sleeping. Questions, questions, questions. Your answers are never enough. Observations about life. Why? When? How? Why, again? The talking goes on and on and on like a hypnotist's medallion and it's about nothing important like: "I'm five years old, that's older than four, two years older than three, and Big Bird is 6 years old — at least that's what the card on the Sesame Street trivia game said - and I can't wait to be six so I can be as old as Big Bird but, Daddy, if you watched Big Bird when you were a kid, and you're O-L-D, is Big Bird really six or is it a lie like when you told me they didn't make Pez Dispensers anymore because I asked Gwace and she said..."

6. CHRISTMAS TREES AND ONE-YEAR-OLDS

There is a fish in the ocean called the Angler Fish. It has this little antenna light that it suspends near its mouth. Little fish are "drawn" to the light and when they get close enough - WHAM! The Angler Fish devours them. To a one-year-old, a Christmas tree is a lot like the Angler Fish - only the tree has 1345 lights, instead of one. There's also the sticky sap issue.

CANTON'S FIRST SWIMMING LESSON:

We traveled to Destin, Florida this summer. It was fun, but I noticed that Canton was the only kid at the beach wearing a life vest. (In addition, Canton is the only kid I currently know that insists on wearing goggles when we wash his hair in the bathtub.) Because of these facts, we decided to enhance his love for water by enrolling him in swimming lessons. So, with his goggles and his

Elmo towel in hand, the whole family arrived at the indoor pool for the first class.

It should be noted, that if I were to use one word to describe Canton's swimming level on day one of the lessons, it would be "Rock." Thus, we enrolled him in the beginner's class called, "Little Guppies." That being said, I'm not sure what kind of guppies are zipping around Missouri waterways, but as we were about to see, apparently they are pretty impressive swimmers.

This particular rec center had a rule that everyone must shower before entering the pool. I forgot this, but noticed all the other children were dripping wet as they sat on the side of the pool. I asked the instructor if Canton needed to shower and her answer consisted of looking at the other soaking wet children one by one. I got the hint and whisked Canton toward the shower. He yelled, "Ahhhhhhh! I don't wanna' get wet!!!!" I heard the other parents chuckle. I agreed. That was hilarious- in an ironic sort of way.

I wrestled Canton into the shower stall and used the hand-held showerhead to wash him down. In the tussle, I sprayed myself in the face - twice. We both returned to the pool – dripping wet – and I saw the other parents chuckle again.

The instructor of the class (Miss Carey) pulled the kids to the middle of the pool and placed them on a makeshift platform of plastic and PVC pipe. I was a little worried - as was Canton - since I've always tried to teach him that, 1) he should be nice to his brother, and 2) PVC pipe is not a floatation device.... Regardless, I whipped out my camera ready to capture a cute moment - maybe blowing bubbles in the pool for the first time. Miss Carey clapped her hands and said, "Okay kids, let's see how long you can hold your breath under water. I will count. Who wants to go first?"

I leaned over to Rana, "*Which* class did you sign him up for?"

Rana: "The beginning class... I think?"

One little, pig-tailed, teacher's-pet-looking-girl, bounced up and down and yelled, "I'll go, Miss Carey!" and, without waiting for a response, proceeded to submerge himself. Miss Carey was counting loudly and was becoming bored as she shouted out, " Sixteen... Seventeen..."

The little girl then exploded out of the water and wiped the water from her eyes, grinning with pride. Miss Carey was very impressed, as was the little girl's mother who was making her way to the edge of the pool to apparently give her daughter a high five. I began to get up with the hope of assisting the mother in joining her daughter in the pool. Rana grabbed my arm.

The whole time Canton was watching. That's actually not accurate… Canton's mouth was hanging down touching the water as he looked at us in horror. Miss Carey pointed at Canton and said, "Okay, you go under now."

Canton nodded hesitantly. (Let's just say Rana and I were skeptical.) He proceeded to spend an exorbitant amount of time tightening his goggles. The goggles were getting tight. Really tight. Canton's head was starting to turn purple. Finally, the goggles were so tight, they sprang off his head and landed in the far end of the pool. Now Canton couldn't use them because there was water on them. Miss Carey waded over to get the goggles and handed them to me to dry off. I hurriedly tried to dry off the goggles on my shirt. All the parents were watching me angrily because class was now half over. I dried the goggles. I tossed them back to Miss Carey. (Miss Carey couldn't catch a cold.) The goggles ricocheted off her brick hands and splashed into the water. Canton yelled, "They're all wet again!" One Dad stood up and looked as if he wanted to do bad things to me. Miss Carey told Canton to go under. He yelled, "Fine!" and began to lower himself. Lower. Lower. Lower... and stopped when his lower lip touched the water. I was pretty impressed and I stood up to cheer. Rana pulled me back onto the bench.

It was interesting to note that Miss Carey was not very attractive. This was only important, not because I wanted to date her, but because it was obvious that Canton was interested in pleasing just the pretty girls. One day, Miss Carey was absent and was replaced by a much prettier instructor. Canton coolly eased his way into the pool, took her arm and said, "Wanna watch me go under the water?"

She smiled and said, "Sure."

Canton proceeded to completely submerge himself (for the first time without his goggles) and came blasting out of the water.

Rana and I just shook our heads. (Gwace will have her work cut out for her.)

CANTON QUOTE

I had been carpooling to school with my friend Josh. One Spring morning, Josh wasn't going to be with us.

Me: "Josh isn't coming with us today."

Canton: "Why not?"

Me: "He's going hunting today."

Canton smiled widely: "Oh, that should be fun for him... Is he hunting Easter eggs?"

ALL ABOUT RANA AND ME:

I graduated with my Master's Degree in Elementary Administration. Glad it's over. Being back in school while you're teaching school can be tough at times. I'm also still coaching Track – with the goal that we can go one whole season without an "athlete" tripping on the hurdles and hurting themselves.

Rana is still working in Child Life at the hospital. Her favorite day comes when the cafeteria serves taco salad. Rana got a new SUV. I need a new car – my steering wheel shakes when I drive too fast. I think I have a leak in my in-ground sprinklers. Montana's lost 10 pounds. I've gained four – or maybe six… That's been our year in a nutshell. As you can see, there's much more interesting things going on with our kids.

TIME TO TIE THIS UP

Rana and I had been looking for a picture to hang on the big wall above our piano. We've been looking for quite some time and no picture, clock, mirror, or wall sconce seemed right. Then, while perusing a shop in Destin, we found it. It's a poem painted by an artist named Bergman on an antique looking wooden surface. Above the poem is a deeply recessed space for a picture. We made a black and white copy of our favorite wedding picture, placed it there. I'm closing this letter with this, because in a sense, the poem is not only about us, but about you as well:

> *What are you doing the rest of your life*
>
> *The East West North and South of your life*
>
> *I only have one request of your life*
>
> *That you spend it all with me*

This year has been a challenge as we've struggled with Rana's Dad's cancer, my Dad's heart surgery, Rana's Mom's eye surgery, and Grandma Post passing away. But as tough as the road sometimes appears, everything always seems to end up okay. That's probably because, in the end, you are all standing right there – spending your lives with us.

We thank you for that. And we thank God for you.

Love and Peace in the coming year

John, Rana, Canton (his wife, Gwace), Harper, and Montana

CHAPTER ELEVEN
Christmas 2007

*Claw Machines, Pacifier Loss
& Brotherly Love*

A Holiday Hello to Everyone!

I sat down in November to write this Christmas letter (I bet you didn't know I could be such a planner), but was interrupted by our dog barking and the very distinct sounds of splashing. I rushed downstairs to find Harper attempting to bathe himself (and the entire kitchen) in Montana's water bowl. After drying Harper off and getting him to bed, Canton convinced Rana and me to play Sesame Street Chutes and Ladders. That game should really be called "Eternity," because just when you think someone might win (and honestly after an hour, you don't care if that person is you - you just want somebody to win, so the game will be over) you land on the stupid slide and head back towards start… Anyway, this is how the rest of 2007 went. We couldn't get anything done in a timely fashion. Well, it's now December 23rd, I am still writing this letter and Rana says she needs to proof it. (I already told her that she didn't need to waste valuable time trying to find grammar mistakes, since I is English teacher for sakes Pete.) So, you may end up reading this letter in 2008, which means I'm "a year late." And truthfully, that's a tad bit embarrassing. So without further delay, we begin…

Okay…rewind to a few weeks after we sent you our last Christmas letter. There was that little issue of the claw machine at Wal-Mart…Remember the plexi-glass box stuffed with junky toys that you try to "grab" with a faulty claw? I have to be honest here - you have a better chance of being killed by a grilled cheese sandwich than actually retrieving a prize from that box. (Some of you, while imagining horrifying scenarios with a grilled cheese sandwich, are now wondering just how little there is to do in our town when the Wal-Mart claw machine is a form of family entertainment and makes it in the Christmas letter two years in a row. My thoughts exactly.)

Anyway, after spending $387.25 worth of his (?) quarters during the year, Canton said we needed to talk. Canton informed me that it was my fault that none of his (?) quarters worked in securing the plush and velvety (pathetic-looking) Big Bird doll from the crane. He said I pressed the button too fast. I was "one hundred thousand gazillion feet off" (Canton is very good at math) in lining up the claw over the helpless stuffed toy. And, finally, apparently I wasn't supposed to hold my breath while inserting (wasting) the quarters in the machine. If I'd only let him do it all by himself, he'd have a stuffed treasure in his possession by now.

Fine.

At Wal-Mart the next day, I handed him his (?) quarter. With a determined gleam in his eye, Canton stared down the claw - two cowboys about to duel in the Wild West.

"Come on, quarter! Go get that Big Bird!" he exclaimed rather loudly - loud enough that several Wal-Mart customers with their carts and even two Wal-Mart employees stopped to watch. Canton slid the quarter into the slot. ("Nice knowing you Quarter # 1513," I mumbled.) Undaunted, Canton cocked his head sideways and squinted. He was determined. The claw would not win. He tugged at the "joystick" and positioned the claw directly over (not even remotely close to) the Big Bird.

"Come on, Big Bird! Come on!" The onlookers seemed to be rooting for him.

Canton looked at Rana and me, as if to ask if it was the right moment to press the red button and lower the crane. Without waiting for any word from us, he turned suddenly and pressed the button. Down, down, down the crane zipped. We all leaned forward.

The crane's claw missed Big Bird completely (though it did graze what I can only describe as a neon, orange elephant-zebra) and began to zip upward. "Oh, no!" Canton yelled. The crowd sighed.

Suddenly, the claw miraculously snagged the tag that was attached to Big Bird's head. It wrapped around the claw, which now had no choice but to carry the Big Bird to the prize chute. (I think I saw the claw actually trying to shake loose the Big Bird, but to no avail.)

To say that Canton freaked out is an understatement. He jammed his hand into the prize door and yanked out his new Big Bird doll. He hugged it tightly and began to spin in circles, like in a movie when two people in love are reunited after years apart.

Canton screamed, "Yes, yes, yes!" at the top of his lungs - while stomping his little feet in euphoria. The people who had stopped to watch began to cheer. They whistled. They clapped. A Wal-Mart employee even slapped a yellow Wal-Mart smiley face sticker on his chest.

One man turned to me, pointed at Canton, and said, "I'd hate to see him in Vegas."

You may be wondering why the claw story is important. Well, I think it symbolized a maturing for Canton. He started kindergarten this year. His claw machine victory prepared him for it. It taught him that there is nothing he cannot do. Unfortunately, the experience has misled him into thinking he also knows EVERYTHING.

Here are a three examples of Kindergarden Canton's insight:

1)   The Post family has (unfortunately) had several vomiting experiences this year. Not to gross you all out during this holiday season, but it was a fascinating topic of conversation for many weeks in our house. Both boys seemed extremely hesitant to eat dinner for fear of getting sick again. (I reassured them that Mommy had promised not to cook our meals for a few weeks.) Anyway, a few days after one of the barfing incidents, we were all sitting at the table eating dinner, and Canton started to get a funny expression on his face. I thought he was going to blow again. I looked at Rana and, in order not to draw any attention, I spelled out part of my sentence:

"Is he gonna' P-U-K-E?" I asked.

"Puke!?!" Canton hollered. "Hey, is that Spanish for 'throw up?'"

2)   I was driving the boys to daycare and school one morning. Harper was saying "I poopy," over and over because he thought that would force me to let him escape from his car seat. (At first I thought it was clever, but very quickly I just wanted him to stop LYING.) Since Canton was not fake-gagging and rolling down the window to clear out a horrendous smell from the car, I knew Harper was indeed lying about the poop.   But, he wouldn't stop saying, "I poopy." Over and over.   And over.   I was losing my patience. (And over.)

That's it! I turned around, pointed at Harper, and hollered, "Canton, cut it out!"

Canton said, "Hey, you called him the wrong name!"

I said, "Sorry. I do that sometimes."

Canton said, "Daddy, you wanna' know why you do that sometimes?"

I have to admit – I was interested. "Yes, Canton, tell me why I sometimes call you guys by the wrong name."

Canton explained, "You get confused because the word 'Canton' and the word 'Harper' both have 'a' as the second letter."

I see.

3)   One last example from Canton Know-it-all: This year, Canton appointed himself the "Who Prays First Director" during the bedtime routine. But instead of saying, "Daddy, you go first" like a normal child, he started describing some quality about the person he wanted to go next. For example:

Daddy: "Who's turn is it to pray?"

Canton: "Whoever has stinky feet!"

Daddy: "Oh, I guess that's me," and Canton would say, "That's riiiightttttttttttt!"

So, one night I said, "Who's going first tonight?"

He started to tap his chin. He was really thinking it over, and then suddenly said, "The person whose idea of a nightmare is a peanut butter and jelly sandwich just out of reach."

After staring blankly at each other, Rana and I realized he was talking about himself.

We imagined that even God chuckled at that one…

While Canton has had the biggest changes this year, 2-year-old Harper has been basically holding his own in the household. He tells the dog what to do, helps himself to toys in his brother's room, and last weekend even yelled, "I poopy" in our friend's bathtub. (God, I *wish* he *had* been lying about that one!) But there have been some changes this year for poor Harper, too. When he turned 2, we decided it was time for him to stop sucking his Binky (pacifier). But we were not totally inhumane. We prepared him for it.

I sat him down and kissed him on the head. In my sweetest voice I said, "Honey, your teeth will be jacked up if you keep sucking on that thing. Plus, do you want people calling you "Pacifier Pants?"

He stared at me with a pouty lip.

Mommy had a better idea. She decided we'd replace Binky with a stuffed animal "friend" that Harper could bond with at night time. (Canton helped us get one out of the Wal-Mart claw machine… Just kidding!)

Rana really played it up. The new friend was going to be named "Binky Dog." She wrapped him up and made Harper bag up his binkies for an even trade. After all of this build up, Harper was so excited to be getting rid of Binky so he could sleep with Binky Dog.

The day of his birthday arrived, and so did the first naptime without his Binky.

Rana handed Harper his Binky Dog. He gasped in glee and hugged him tightly. Then he said, "Gimmie Bink."

"No, honey. You are a big boy now. Remember you traded your binky for Binky Dog."

"I no wannit," Harper said, his brow wrinkling.

"But, you *love* Binky Dog," Rana insisted.

"No!" he yelled and threw poor Binky Dog across the room, where it hit the wall with a thud (Arf!).

Needless to say, it took a lot of crying (Mommy, Daddy and Harper) to get good at falling asleep without Binky.

About 2 months later - Binky a distant memory - we were walking in a children's store, trying to pick up a friend's baby shower present. Harper was trailing behind us, when we heard an enormous gasp.

We whirled around to see Harper pointing up, with his mouth hanging open. Over fifty brand new binkies were hanging on hooks. It must have looked like sparkling glasses of water to a man in a desert. It was hard to distract him and move him away from the display...I think it was the giant Elmo balloon bouquet we had to purchase that allowed us to get him out of there without incident. Now - we have to go visit that store to say "hi" to the binkies. Binky Dog lives in Harper's crib now, but is an unloved observer in the corner. Honestly, the dead roly poly that Harper insists on leaving in his bed seems to get more attention. (We know. That's gross.)

Speaking of bugs... (I'm ashamed of that weak transition, but it's now midnight and that's all I've got left in the tank.) Harper loves bugs. He likes to touch them, stomp them, and even taste them if they aren't moving too fast (See: roly poly above.) So, when Canton got a book called *Bugs! Bugs! Bugs!* as a gift, I was excited to read it to the budding entomologist. The book had a menacing, extra-large Praying Mantis on the cover. Rana seemed hesitant, as she sat on the floor next to me.

"Have you read this before?" she asked.

"Uh, no," I replied smartly. "But, I'm pretty sure I'll be able to handle it." She tilted her head sideways. (Every man reading this knows exactly what that means, but since this is a "family" publication, I won't type it out here.)

Harper was sitting between my legs, and he was pretty excited about this book. He was pointing at the scary bug on the front cover and shouting: "Bug!" rather jubilantly. Canton was standing behind me - leaning over my shoulder - perhaps because he was scared of the bug on the cover...

I began on page 1 where there was a picture of a red ant: "Yikes. Bugs look scary up close. But you don't need to worry..." (See, Mommy? Nothin' to worry about.)

Harper was really listening intently, and Canton was telling me I did a good job reading that first page. Apparently, it was pretty difficult.

I flipped the page and was greeted by a zoomed in picture of a very frightening insect's jaws. It seemed like it might be chewing on something - like six or seven legs of a caterpillar. I continued: "Some bugs hunt other bugs..." (*Where are we going with this?* I asked myself.)

Page 3: "The assassin bug is a bug that really lives up to its name. An assassin is a person who kills another person on purpose." (Oh, crap.)

Canton: "Why does he kill, Daddy?"

Harper: "Kwill?"

Mommy: "Story time's over boys. Daddy just lost his book choosing privileges."

As you can see, parenthood is not an exact science. Rana and I used to joke that she would raise the kids until they were teenagers, with me taking over from that point on. It seemed like that would be ideal, since I teach teenage, middle schoolers and she likes babies. (The confusing part about that arrangement is that babies don't act like middle schoolers, but middle schoolers can definitely act like babies.) In the meantime, I try to help out as best I can.

Truthfully, it doesn't seem like my parenting "assistance" has messed up our boys' too much. They still seem to still like both of their parents and, in reality, they both seem to get along well with each other. But, as in all great relationships, there are times when brotherly bothering, bantering, berating, and bickering are inevitable. Here are a couple of examples:

*Harper had been sent to Time Out at Grandma's about 4 straight days. There seemed to be a pattern occurring. Canton was well aware of this pattern. It was a perfect time to strike with fake philanthropy!

Canton: "Hey, Harper. Did you go to Time Out today at Grandma's?"

Harper: "Yes."

Canton: "Oh, that's too bad (insert overly-dramatic sad face here). If you hadn't gone to Time Out, I would've given you my favorite Big Bird doll."

Yeah right!

*Harper loves to be in his brother's room. Canton isn't so keen on that idea. Ever. But Harper keeps on knocking, and Canton keeps on ignoring him.

One day after ten straight minutes of knocking, I heard a bedroom door swing open, and Canton yelled, "Here!"

Harper gasped, giggled, then yelled, "Tank you brudder!" and ran down the hall with a piece of paper clenched in his hand.

"Harper, what's that in your hand?" I asked.

Harper replied, "Brudder's note!"

"You got a note from brother?"

Grinning from ear to ear, he exclaimed, "Yes!"

I took the note. Scribbled lovingly on the paper, the words: "YOU KEEP OUT!"

Oh, brother.

*At the dinner table: Harper was goofing-off and squishing mac-n-cheese between his lips and letting in dribble down his chin. We were trying to ignore him.

Canton looked at us, quite disgusted, and said, "I didn't ask for this."

Rana: "You didn't ask for what?"

"This brother," he says, pointing at Harper.

(And we get it. Harper is sweet, but he DOES have the table manners of an iguana.)

Most of you are going cross-eyed, so it's time to tie it up with a story. Harper gets the honors this year...

We were driving, and Harper had this finger-painted, paper plate turkey he made at daycare. He was holding it by the popsicle stick glued to the back and waving it to the music. He was grinning from ear to ear.

Harper said, "Mommy, wook at me."

Rana turned around and smiled, "What?"

"Happy," he grinned - still waving his turkey.

She said, "Oh, is your turkey happy?"

"No," he smiled. "*I* happy."

Enough to melt your heart. And I think that's where we are right now. Just happy. We are so blessed - our lives filled to the brim with each other and all of you. We couldn't ask for more. Thank you for making our life so fantastically full.

May God bless you this year. We love you!

John, Rana, Canton, Harper, Montana (and Binky D.)

CHAPTER TWELVE
Christmas 2008

*Tooth Fairies, Bad Words at School
& Bike Riding 101*

Feliz Navidad,

Rana and I were tag-teaming this letter, when we heard whimpering.

We clambered downstairs and found Canton sitting on his bed - in the dark - rubbing his eyes. Rana sat down on the bed and asked him what was wrong.

"I had a nightmare," he sniffed.

"Oohh," Rana said and put her arm around him consolingly.

I asked, "What was the nightmare about, bud?"

"I dreamed there was dog food in my underwear."

Yikes! That IS scary. Almost as scary as the thought of hardly having started The Christmas Letter. So while Mommy rubbed his back and hummed a song, I rushed back upstairs to write the letter...but sadly, the TV was on. Sports. ESPN. Like most men, I was powerless to resist its seductive charms. There would be no Christmas letter this night. (Instead, I enjoyed watching a fantastic Neon/Lights-Out Bowling Tournament - in which strobe lights peppered the blacked-out lanes and the glowing, pink pins really seemed to be giving the bowlers fits. Very amusing.)

It's now three days later and I've returned to the computer. (No, the bowling tourney didn't last that long - but there were other sports that kept coming on and distracting me.) Apparently, our lives have been very busy – and watching sports has been one of the culprits... Also, I've decided it's difficult to find time to type Christmas letters when you're making so many millions each day playing the stock market. Okay, that joke was in poor taste – especially if you, like us and so many others - got creamed by the stock market this year.

Truth be told, we're *not* making millions in the stock market. But, on a related note, if I had a quarter for every time this past month I picked up my cell phone and said, "Touch your brother one more time, and I'm calling Santa," I would be a millionaire. (Side note: I would be roughly $600,000 richer if I had a quarter for each time this month I've said, "Stop blowing bubbles in your milk and farting.")

It's one of the things they never tell you in the parenting magazines: December is the easiest month of the year for parents. Currently, I don't even have to say the word "Santa." I just pick up my phone and look at them. Unfortunately, this has caused rampant paranoia in my children... Yesterday, I picked up the phone to order a pizza, and Harper jumped off the couch and yelled, "Please don't call Santa!"

While December parenting has been easy, the year as a whole has been slightly difficult because Harper decided 2008 was the perfect time to grow an opinion. It just so happens, that lucky for us (sarcasm), his opinion is always the exact opposite of anything we want him to do. If we want him to wear a coat, he wants to run into the garage naked. If we want him to eat his dinner, he wants to surprise the dog with a spaghetti shower falling from the sky. And if we want him to go to bed...SERIOUSLY?!

He's now fond of saying things are "stupid." We don't like that word - except when referring to any team playing the Mizzou Tigers...

Harper: "Canton, you're stupid!"

Rana: "Harp, we don't call our brother stupid."

Harper: "But, he *is* stupid."

Harper also likes the word, "hate." Mostly it's **bedtime** that has enhanced his affinity for that word. We don't like the word 'hate,' either. We think it's stupid.

Me: "Eat your corn, please."

Harper, scrunching up his nose: "I *hate* corn. It smells like stinky socks."

Me: "We don't say 'hate.'"

Harper, throwing up his arms: "I *hate* that we don't say hate!"

In direct correlation with Harper's new-found opinion, Canton turned 7. That means he's become more perfect than perfect. Personal flaws are gone. Imperfections are a thing of the past. Rana and I are wrong - even when we're right. And in his view, life in other houses might just be preferable.

I know this because the other day, Canton arrived home from 1st grade. He was very excited and wore a gigantic grin as he proclaimed that he just loved his teacher, Mrs. Sevon.

He then asked, "Can I marry Mrs. Sevon?"

Me: "No, because she's already married."

"That's too bad," Canton shook his head. "I guess I'm stuck here with you guys."

Apparently, in the past year, Rana and I have also become embarrassing to our oldest son.

At some point while shopping, we noticed our boys were losing the ability to act like normal humans. Finally, after the 105th skirmish, I decided to keep shopping with Harper while Rana took

Canton to the car. As she pulled him (not gently) by the hand through the parking, their conversation went something like this:

Canton: "Why are we going to the car, Mommy?"

Mommy: "Because, you were running around like a wild man and it was really embarrassing."

10 seconds pass.

Canton: "Well, *you're* embarrassing *me* by dragging me to the car like this!"

Since this letter is transitioning so beautifully between seemingly random topics, I'm going to continue the trend. I'll start the next paragraph by saying I hate (oops) - dislike the Tooth Fairy. Please allow me to explain:

Last month, Canton lost his first tooth at school. When I picked him up, he nearly tackled me - while shoving his pearly white toward my face. Gross.

We were driving home and he was grinning like a banker - albeit a toothless one.

I looked in the rear view mirror and said, "What are you grinning about?"

Canton said, "Now, the Tooth Fairy will give me money!"

"That's right, she *will*," I agreed. I wrinkled my brow as I felt in my pocket and found I had no money. Not one stinkin' dollar. I looked at the clock and realized the bank was closed for the day. Dang it!

Canton said, "How much money will the Tooth Fairy give me, Dad?"

"Uh…" (I scanned my memory banks to my own childhood, and *purposely* ignoring obvious inflation, said, "One dollar.")

Canton asked, "One dollar? That's *it?* That's not fair. Hannah got $3 from the Tooth Fairy!"

I had a hard time believing this because Hannah's dad, Eric, was a great friend of mine and I knew he was much too sensible to throw $3 at a dead tooth. I decided to call him to file a complaint.

Ring, ring, ring…

Eric: "Hello?"

Me: "Hey, Daddy Warbucks…I heard the Tooth Fairy at your house gave Hannah 3 bucks for her first lost tooth. Thanks a lot, pal!"

Eric laughed out loud. He said, "We didn't know how much to give either! I had three bucks in my pocket, so we just gave her that. The next day, I told my co-workers. They all thought I gave too much. I think one buck is still the going rate. So, now we're hosed for every other Tooth Fairy visit."

"I guess we are too," I said. "We really appreciate your generosity," I laughed and hung up.

I turned back toward Canton. "Okay, I guess you're right. The Tooth Fairy will *probably* be giving you $3."

"Great," Canton nodded. "I sure hope she gives it to me in quarters, so I can try them in the claw machine. (No, you're not imagining things. This is the third consecutive year the Christmas letter has made reference to the stupid [er, sorry] Wal-Mart claw machine.)

After Canton went to sleep - with strict instructions to wake him when the Tooth Fairy arrived - I went to Wal-Mart and got some quarters. Now I want you to picture me, Daddy Tooth Fairy,

139

pixy-dusting my way into a pitch black room, tip-toing around the approximately 36 Big Bird dolls Canton had arranged on the floor like land mines to greet me. I also want you to imagine a little boy clutching his pillow with both arms - because he told me (and I quote) "I want her money, but I don't want her to take my tooth." I was trying to keep the 12 quarters from making a jingling sound in my hand, and I was using my cell phone for "light." How I got the 12 quarters under his pillow is beyond me. How I escaped his room without crushing any of his Big Bird dolls was equally miraculous.

(You're probably wondering if Canton won anything with his quarters. Of course he did - a large stuffed Winnie the Pooh. The kid's gifted.)

In addition to losing teeth, Canton may have also lost some of his innocence by hearing some "Bad Words at School."

Rana met the boys and me at Applebee's for dinner, when Canton sprung this story on us. Canton's kindergarten teacher had been out on maternity leave and had just returned.

I said, "Did Mrs. Tanner have a good first day back?"

"No," Canton shook his head. "Her day was *horrible*."

Harper was staring at his brother.

Rana: "Why was her day horrible?"

Canton: "Because Ethan said bad things to her."

Rana and I looked at each other. (Okay, I had to ask…)

Me: "What bad things did Ethan say?" I squinted my eyes a bit - preparing for the reply.

Canton, very casually: "Ethan said the B-word. And also the N-word to Mrs. Tanner."

Rana and I went wide-eyed. Harper was still silent and watching, barely breathing.

I leaned across the table, cupped my hand to my ear, and asked, "What's the B-word and the N-word?"

Canton picked up a French fry and took a big bite. He then shook his head - like he didn't want to get in trouble for saying them out loud.

"You're not going to be in trouble," Rana promised, holding her hands over Harper's ears. "Just tell Daddy what Ethan said."

He finished chewing, swallowed loudly and said, "Naked... and... Butt!"

I nearly spit out my soda.

"Oh *good!*" I exclaimed.

"Dad, it's *not* good," Canton scolded. "It was horrible. Mrs. Tanner was *very* sad about it."

Me: "Oh. I'm sorry."

Hearing bad words at school was certainly a sign that our eldest child was growing up too fast. But perhaps the ultimate sign that Canton was "breaking the bonds of childhood innocence" came when he had to learn how to ride his bike without training wheels for the first time.

A little background info: Because my wife works with hospitalized children, she describes herself as a "Safety Geek." Thus, she takes (many, a lot, a ton of) precautions to prevent our children from being injured. Our boys will never have the joy of breaking their arm on a trampoline (we will never own one), hitting a tree on a 4-wheeler (we will never own one), or shooting their brother with a rocket launcher (we can't afford one due to the stupid stock market).

The boys *are* allowed, however, to ride bikes - an activity we enjoy as a family nearly every evening in the summer. During these times we've noticed that our boys seem to be the only children in the neighborhood who wear their helmets when they ride with us. They actually love their helmets so much that they like to wear them even when they aren't riding bikes. They like to wear them when we walk the dog, for example. Adults in our neighborhood drive by slowly and watch our boys running down the sidewalk with their safety helmets on - and shake their heads sadly. Once, Harper even tried to take a nap in his helmet. It wasn't allowed with Safety Geek on the job. Chin strap choking hazard, you know? In addition, Harp couldn't quite seem to get comfortable...

Anyway, we loved to ride bikes as a family, Rana and I towing our children in a bike trailer. But it wasn't long before they got too tall to ride in the trailer safely - plus, on windy days – it felt like I was towing a dual door refrigerator. So, now Rana and I would just walk around the neighborhood· together - Harper rumbling along on his police big wheel and Canton riding gingerly on his John Deere bike with training wheels. When Harper began doing figure 8's around his brother, I decided Canton's training wheels had to go.

Canton was a *little* hesitant when I suggested removing the training wheels.

(Canton:
"Nooooooooooooooooooooooooooooooooooooo!!!!!!!!!!!!")

Me: "Come on. I'll keep you from falling."

I even put on my helmet for safety's sake.

It took a few weeks, but Canton figured out how to go straight. He couldn't turn, but that would come with time. Once

142

convinced he could do it, we went further away from the driveway. Canton insisted that he couldn't ride that far without falling.

"You'll be fine," I said as I pushed him toward the driveway.

My choice to wheel out the large, blue trash bin to the curb that morning proved ill-advised.

Canton couldn't turn the bike and ran face first into the trash can.

There were bruises, but the trash can didn't cry. Canton did.

"I'll NEVER ride again!" he bawled.

That happened at the end of the summer. So, we spent September trying to plant nice riding thoughts in his head. We even tried to catch a few Tour De France replays on ESPN to show Canton there was nothing to be afraid of and that riding bikes was awesome. And, as I pointed out to him, unlike The Tour, when riding at our house, there wasn't any inconvenient testing of banned human growth hormone.

Speaking of growth hormone, Harper is a BIG man on campus now. He started preschool. He loves it and his teacher, Mrs. Jenny. We were a little worried about how he was going to cope with the whole thing, but now that he's settling in, he is learning lots of valuable life lessons. For instance, one day after returning from school, he proudly told Grandma, "We don't say butt cheeks!"

Harper's way into sports. I knew we were in trouble, when I walked upstairs and found him with one of my posters rolled up. He had it standing vertically and had a rubber ball on top. He was using it as a t-ball stand, as he swung his plastic bat with all his might. Yep - we're going to be busy!

In terms of fashion, Harper will only wear lime green Crocs and shirts with #s on them. His favorite is his Mizzou #10 Chase

Daniel football jersey that he wants to wear all the time. I think it's cute, but sometimes smells stinky. Like corn.

Canton is also doing well in school. He doesn't tell me directly, but I gather as much by listening to him on the way home from school, as he reenacts the day from the back seat:

Canton: "Okay class, who knows how to spell 'buffalo?' Class? Anyone? Anyone at all? Canton Post? Oh, Canton. You're wonderful. Of course you know how to spell 'buffalo.' You can spell anything! You're the smartest boy in class. Class? Don't you wish you were as smart as Canton? He's the greatest boy. You all need to act like him. He's very polite and reads books bestest…"

And on and on and on… Though I'm sure he's exaggerating, listening to him recap his day without me having to ask is almost as entertaining as watching Neon Bowling.

Canton has decorated his room at home in a classroom theme. He's got the "school" calendar and Words of the Day up all over his walls. Canton says he wants to be a teacher when he grows up. That makes me proud. He says he also wants to be a Wal-Mart claw machine operator in the evenings, weekends and summers. He says he won't make the toys so "smashed down" so more kids can win them.

In terms of Rana and I, we've been busy. I found out I have to have disc fusion surgery on my neck next week. I don't know how I hurt it - maybe while contorting my body to get the quarters under Canton's pillow? I still love teaching but I resigned from coaching track. I was then asked to coach Cross Country. I agreed because Cross Country is like Track without the whining - since the kids who join actually *like* to run long distances.

Rana's doing well too. She had to fire her first employee. They say that's the first step in mastering upper level management.

Rana and a (non-fired) co-worker are looking into getting their MBA's very soon.

Well, it's time to tie this thing up...I'm going to close with a line I heard recently in a Christmas movie: "When happiness shows up, make sure you give it a comfortable seat." At this time of year, we really reflect on how lucky we are - especially to have all of you in our lives. And even though we're not making millions in the stock market, we truly could not be happier. A comfy seat indeed. Thank you for being such a special part of our family. May God bless you with overflowing happiness this year.

Love,

Daddy Tooth Fairy, Rana,
Canton, and Harp
(plus, Montana the dog)

CHAPTER THIRTEEN
Christmas 2009

*Wild World of Sports Truly Begins &
We Need Another Dog?!*

Ho Ho Ho (For some reason, that doesn't seem like a very appropriate way to begin a Christmas letter),

Well, you are lucky to be getting a letter this year, because it just took us one month to set up our Christmas tree. This time frame was a direct result of our children "helping" us.

Harper, bless his little heart, hasn't quite gotten the hang of hanging ornaments yet. From five ornaments on the same branch, to hanging ornaments on the light cord, to heavy ornaments hanging on the carpet because they were attached to the lowest, weakest branches, we had to go behind him and fix his decorating gaffs. The only good thing was that since he's only four years old, we needn't look for "ornament errors" on any branches higher than 28 inches off the ground.

Canton, on the other hand, wanted every ornament he had ever made or had ever been given, to hang front and center on our tree for everyone to see. We thought we had fixed this problem when we bought him his own 3 foot tree to smother with as many Sesame Street and popsicle stick ornaments as his little heart desired. But his tree filled up too quickly (and subsequently fell over from the weight of ceramics) and now our tree had become the target of his leftover "uglyments." Though I'm ashamed (a little) to admit this, I convinced Canton that his ornaments (such as the shriveled, puke-green and pink-swirled, twice-baked, candy cane that may have been chewed on by a former classmate) should be on the side of the tree facing the window so the whole neighborhood could see them as they drove by. He liked that idea - eventually.

As we sat down to recover, Rana reminded me that we didn't have much time to rest because the Christmas letter deadline was nearing. Then, the phone rang. It was the rec center trying to set up Harper's first basketball practice. What perfect material (sports) for our letter this year! So, without further delay...

The Wild World of Sports in the Post house began like this:

149

Grandma: "Harper, are you going to take swimming lessons this summer?"

"No," Harper said, crinkling his brow.

"Why not?" Grandma asked.

"I love the swimming, but I don't really like the *sinking*," he said.

Stifling a laugh, Grandma asked, "Well, then what are you going to play?"

"Oh, Grandma, you're gonna' be so excited for me! I'm gonna' play baseball, soccer, tennis, and football. And golf. And also basketball, but I'm kinda' short."

So starting at the beginning of the list, we signed Harper up for YMCA T-ball. We bought him a mini-glove and began practicing each day. He was starting to get the hang of catching - grounders and even pop-ups. But according to him, the only thing keeping him from being the "bestest player" was the fact that the "dumb sun" kept getting in his eyes. Therefore, he was forced to wear his blue and yellow fish sunglasses - specifically designed for the beach. We promised that we'd get him some new, sportier sunglasses soon. He was satisfied with that.

Then, the afternoon of the first practice arrived and Harper seemed distressed. I asked him what was wrong.

"I need sunglasses, so I can catch the ball today," he said.

"Okay, go get them," I said. He smiled widely, then disappeared around the corner in search of sunglasses.

As I was filling water bottles in the kitchen, Rana was taking a shower (We must be a pretty T-ball mom, you know?). I suddenly heard Harper yell from our bedroom.

I ran in and saw that he had his head tilted wayyy back and Rana's bra draped over his face.

I said, "What *in the world* are you doing?!"

He growled, "I can't see out of these new sunglasses!"

I pulled the bra off of his face and told him, "That's mommy's."

Harper said, "These are *mommy's* new sunglasses?!"

We didn't have time for that conversation, so it was off to our first T-ball practice!

T-ball was the first "organized" sport Harper had played. ("Organized" is in quotes because it wasn't.) For those who are interested, tiny tot T-ball is basically composed of the following 3 components:

1) Mothers snapping pictures like the paparazzi

2) Constant pointers from fathers who all had apparently made significant contributions to Major League Baseball

3) 200 thirsty, hungry, whiny, sunshine yellow t-shirt wearing little people, swinging plastic bats in a chaotic motion - imagine MANY **blindfolded** children whiffing at a piñata.

When we arrived, the kids were divided into groups named after major league baseball teams. How cute. Harper was on the Royals. After watching the first practice, I don't think it was coincidence that Harper's team was named after the Kansas City Royals, who currently stink majorly.

The practice consisted of many "skill" stations and lasted from 6:00 - 7:00pm. A police siren was blared through a megaphone when everyone was supposed to move to the next station. And every time it went off, everyone in attendance literally jumped.

We had just left the "running the bases" station, and I was pretty happy to be moving along. That's because Harper seemed to think he was within the rules of T-ball etiquette when he tackled the chubby kid who hadn't left first base when he arrived.

The throwing station was reasonably entertaining since several kids thought it was more fun to throw their baseball glove at the coach instead of just the ball...

Next stop: Hitting (or hoping to make contact with) the ball off of the tee. I stood back and watched as the yellow kids made a line (sort of) next to the tee. First up, a girl named Emory.

"Go ahead, Emory, hit it," her father said, nudging her forward.

Emory stepped toward the tee and nearly chopped off her own foot with the plastic bat. She swung again. The bat flew out of her hands and helicoptered over the head of the hitting coach.

The dad shook his head.

"Solid swing," I said encouragingly. The girl smiled. The dad looked at me like I had three heads.

"You know what?" he asked.

I stared ahead, without really responding. He mistook my silence for interest and kept talking.

"My girl's only three. She can talk like a ten year old - but sheesh - she's as unathletic as her mother." He nudged me with his elbow and pointed at his wife who was snapping pictures of her daughter. (He was correct. His wife looked the opposite of athletic.)

Then everyone was startled by a cute blonde haired boy (I swear it wasn't Harper) who yelled, "I have to pee sooooo bad!"

152

Then, another cute blonde haired boy yelled, "I have to pee, too!" (Okay, that one was Harper).

Within seconds, every member of the team was pulling at the front of their shorts and screaming about peeing. Luckily, the police siren went off. Every child jumped and sprinted to the next station.

The final station involved the children working on TWO skills at once. The kids got to hit the ball AND run around the bases. It was quite a sight. As the ball was hit and the children ran with the bats, all the parents present yelled as loud as they could, "DROP THE BAT! DROP IT!!!!!" This caused a startling flinging motion by the children and a dangerous situation for all spectators within 50 feet.

I turned my head to the left and saw two kids being pulled up the grassy hill toward the parking lot by an angry mom.

During the hour long practice, I saw at least 6 kids cry. Two fathers did. One child tried to catch the ball with his face. One peed his shorts. A YMCA employee was thumped in the forehead with a flying plastic bat. One kid was stung by a bee. Two parents got into a yelling match. One YMCA referee quit.

At 7:00, there was a sweaty yellow stampede up the grassy hill to the parking lot. Two kids tripped and rolled back down the hill. It was pretty steep.

All these practices prepared the children for the end-of-season World Series. But it wasn't really a series. It was just one game. Yep, one glorious game.

Harper only had 5 other kids on his team that showed up, so before game time, we had a transaction that merged his team with the Padres. This created a normal sized team of about 10 kids that we'll call the Royalpadres. (I'm not referring to stately Hispanic priests - but having some of those on Harper's team would have probably helped.)

Harper's team was supposed to be , playing against the Yankees. The Yankees already had 13 kids but the YMCA folks thought to make it fair, they should merge the Yankees with the Cardinals - making a massive mosh pit of 25 kids we'll call the Yankeenals. And yes, they were all on the field at the same time.

Now, I'm not one of those parents who make excuses when their kids are outperformed by other kids, but I have zero doubt some of those 4-year-old Yankeenals were injecting some kind of giraffe stimulant.

Harper got to bat twice and both times ripped the ball. Unfortunately, the wall of 25 players and their parents made making it safely to first base quite difficult.

Another problem: each time Harper hit the ball and dropped the bat, he didn't even run toward first base. He chased his own ball directly into the field of play. While he had a hard time making it safely to first, he did enjoy making new friends on the dusty pitcher's mound with several members of the Yankeenals.

The game ended in a tie. (I think?) Every kid who played got a medal at the end - which was nice. Even Emory, who swung 7 times and only succeeded in knocking down the plastic t-stand. After the seventh whiff, the YMCA coach just smacked the ball off the tee with his own hand and told her to run. She did and everyone cheered.

Canton wanted to play sports, too. So, he started "organized" tennis lessons in the summer. "Organized" is in quotes because I put Harper's organized T-ball in quotes and I didn't want Canton to feel left out.

I bought Canton a new racket and we even had our first father/son lesson at the courts near our house. That session didn't go very smoothly as Canton didn't think his father - who won a state

Catholic title in high school for Pete's sake - had much valuable tennis info to offer. He also didn't think I was being very patient (Who me?).

I explained I just wanted him to listen to me so he could successfully hit the ball back over the net.

"I know what I'm doing!" he hollered, and grabbing a ball, attempted to hit it with all his might. The ball dribbled harmlessly away. On a positive note, his racket *did* fly over the net.

In spite of my lack of success with his first lesson, Canton was ready for what he called his first **real** tennis lesson at Cooper Tennis Complex. His excitement grew when he saw a smiling Coach Amanda in her tiny-tennis skirt approaching the court with a shopping cart full of tennis balls. Coach Amanda was "relatively cute." ("Relatively cute" is in quotes because it is fun to put words in quotes and my wife is reading this.)

Anyway, Canton's first day consisted of several mini-skill lessons. First skill: the kids balanced a tennis ball on the still racket without the ball rolling off and hitting the ground. Easy schmeezy.

It was after that exercise that one "stocky" boy, wiped his sweatband-covered arm across his brow, set his racket down on the court, and began walking toward the bleachers.

Coach Amanda said, "Hey, where are you going?"

"I'm tired and thirsty," the boy said.

"We *just* started," she said.

"I know but that was **a lot**," the boy said.

Coach Amanda continued without him. Next skill station: kids pushed the ball around the court with their rackets. Simple enough. Coach Amanda then had the kids bounce the ball about 5 inches high on their racket. Gotcha so far. Bouncing the ball on the court with their racket was a slightly more difficult task - and it showed as balls were ricocheting around like bullets and one mom actually took cover behind the bleachers.

Then Coach Amanda said, "Okay this next one is tricky. Wrap your arm around the back of your legs, put your racket between your legs, and bounce the ball on your racket without moving the racket from between your legs." Say what?

It wasn't pretty. Kids were falling on the court trying to get the racket between their legs. Some kids, like Canton, were successful in getting the racket between their legs. He was also successful in striking himself in an uncomfortable way due to the strategic placement of the racket. Balls were literally flying everywhere (No - not those kind - get your mind out of the gutter.)

Coach Amanda looked at the parents on the bleachers and said, "Well, I'm done here. You guys can practice this with your kids at home." Super.

As the weeks went by, Canton really started to get the hang of hitting the ball over the net (without the racket traveling along with it) and the stocky boy gained enough endurance to make it through 3 full skill stations before resting. We were all impressed.

Last sports story, I promise...I was actually done with this Christmas letter, until I went to Harper's first basketball practice tonight. I knew we were in for an "interesting" season when the coach showed up for the first practice and the first thing he said was, "My name is Tory and I have no idea what I'm doing. So if any of you parents want to help me that would be great." Now, I'm not asking a volunteer coach to be Michael Jordan, but having some clue about the game of basketball should be a requirement for the job.

Tory started by doing toe touches and arm raises. (What was this, a PE class from 1963?) He then told the kids they needed to "get in shape" so they started doing wind sprints. For Harper, who loves to run non-stop, this was fun. For the several kids who had done nothing but eat corndogs in the off-season, this wasn't enjoyable. There were hands on hips, and there was some crying. There were also tears-a-plenty during bounce passing drills, when the real basketballs popped most members of the team in the face.

Even though he had reserved the court for a full hour, after 28 minutes, Tory rounded up all the kids.

"That's enough for a first practice," Tory said, clapping his hands together. "Now we have the most important part of practice - picking a team name. Now what do you all want the name to be?"

Tory's daughter piped up, "Daddy, I want to be called the 'Shooting Stars!'"

"Great idea," he said, then realizing favoritism would be frowned upon, looked at the other kids.

Harper raised his hand and said, "I want to be called the Mizzou Tigers!" He then turned to me and gave a thumbs up sign. (I swear I didn't set him up to that, though several parents in attendance looked at my Mizzou sweatshirt and hat and rolled their eyes.)

One kid shouted, "I want to be called the Duncan Mitchells."

Tory said, "That's your name. We can't be named after you - this is a *team* sport."

The kids just looked around at each other.

Tory continued, "Come on kids, we need a team name that's intimidating." (I laughed as I stared at these 4 year old boys pulling wedgies from their shorts, and little pig-tailed girls whispering secrets to each other on the foul line.)

One girl raised her hand shyly and said, "I want to be called The Splash Pops."

Then, all the kids started yelling and jumping up and down. Wow, it was unanimous. So, Harper is now the starting point guard for the (scarily intimidating) Blue Splash Pops of Republic, Missouri.

In spite of how much our kids seem to love sports, I'm not sure either wants to be a professional athlete when they grow up. Canton is convinced he will be a teacher. I asked Harper, if he wanted to be a teacher like his brother and he said, "No, I wanna' be a turtle." So we're aiming high in the Post house.

Speaking of animals… (That was a pitiful transition.)

My buddy Josh found an abandoned beagle puppy running around near our school. I went to his office to see the pup. Looking back, that was a mistake. He was cute. (The beagle, not Josh. Though Josh has a handsome quality.) The dog had these floppy ears. I went home and told Rana we should adopt him.

Rana said, "We already have a dog."

Now, an intelligent man would have taken this statement from his wife and understood the obvious meaning. I was about to prove I was *not* that man.

Without asking Rana, I convinced Josh to "surprise" us by bringing the beagle to our house. (His exact quote to me was, "Didn't Rana say you already had a dog?") Against his better judgement, Josh brought the beagle over and Canton and Harper instantly fell in love. My wife just stared at me.

The pup had no name, so the boys chased him around giggling, "Come here little sweet doggie." I thought that was almost as cute as the floppy ears.

My wife, however, was not impressed with his ears. She was concerned that our dog, Montana, didn't seem to appreciate the enjoyment the beagle gained from spring-boarding off his head.

Despite the growling, nipping, and Montana's raised hackles, I thought the session went well.

Josh left with the puppy so we could talk about adopting him.

"I think Montana needs a friend," I said.

"I think this is an awful idea," she said. (Subtle message missed again.)

I convinced Rana to give it a weekend trial. In hopes of making the trial a permanent gig, I dropped $200 on updated shots and a new doggie bed and kennel.

And that first 24 hours was pure magic. The pup slept the whole night, curled up – kind of draped across Montana's face.

We woke up the next morning to the sound of floppy ears next to our bed. Just precious.

That day, during a family walk, as the pup pranced alongside of Montana, Rana came up with his name: Truman, after Mizzou's mascot. It was a beautiful moment, and the boys cheered. My wife took my hand and kissed my cheek, as she apparently finally realized that I had made the right choice for our family.

That night, Truman woke us up at 12:45 AM. And 1:30. And 4:00. I took him outside each time, but he wouldn't pee. Each time, I carried him back to Montana's bed and he fell asleep.

I started my next morning by stepping in a wet spot in the living room. Then another one...I'm not going to drag out the details of the next 3 weeks, but they involved: The devil dog peeing on the carpet daily, chewing up Canton's toys, pooping in the living room, throwing up in my car, howling at neighborhood dogs that Montana didn't even know were there, and flopping those damn ears to wake us up three times a night.

I called Josh to tell him I couldn't keep this up (If I wanted to remain married). Luckily his cousin, Billy, had a grandmother who had just lost her beagle of 15 years. She was looking for a new one. I said she could have the devil- (er, Truman) for free. Plus, she could have the new kennel and all supplies if she wanted them. A great deal for her - but a BETTER deal for me.

So Billy picked up the dog on a Sunday and by Monday had fallen in love with him - like we had. He slept at the foot of their bed, licked their faces when they woke up, and those floppy ears!

Billy "had the beagle fever bad" and he called Josh on his way to work Tuesday morning: "We've been talking about it and this is the sweetest, most well-behaved dog we've ever seen. John must be c-r-a-z-y. We've decided we're going to keep him and we'll get Grandma another dog."

Later that afternoon, Billy got a call at work. It was his neighbor.

"Hey, Billy, do you by any chance have a new beagle?" the neighbor asked.

"Yeah, why?" Billy asked.

The neighbor said, "Well, the only thing I can figure is your beagle climbed up on your picnic table, jumped over the privacy fence into my yard, came into my house through our doggie door and peed and pooped all over my living room. Plus, he had our dog pinned under the kitchen table."

I'm not going to drag out the details of the next few days, but Billy experienced similar problems that we did - though he didn't waste 3 weeks before he did something about them.

Truman is now living with Billy's grandma and has yet to have an accident in her house. Maybe that's because she allows him to sleep in her bed and cooks him 3 square meals a day and allows him to eat with her at the kitchen table?

I will add that pulling a cute pup away from two little boys comes with a cost. I had to agree to buy the boys their own little 3 gallon aquariums. (So now we have three pets instead of two?)

And it didn't take long before I was forced to admit I have a real problem. Admitting you have a problem is the first step in any healing process. So, I'll just say it: I am an aquarium fish killer. I don't mean to kill them, but so far we've lost all six starter fish and Harper's tank is currently empty. Canton's fish is the only one still hanging on. And I'm not a Math guy, but a 7 out of 8 fatality rate is poor no matter how you break the numbers down.

***

Well, this 2009 Post Family Christmas letter needs to be tied up, so I'll end with a lesson of sorts that I learned over the summer:

I was sweating like a madman, trying to tug up some stupid dandelion tufts, before the wind got them and blew them all over my yard.

Harper came up behind me and asked, "Whatcha' doin' Daddy?"

I grunted, "I'm pulling these stinkin' dandelions out of my yard."

Harper said, "Those aren't dandelions, Daddy."

Without looking up I said, "Yes they are."

Harper said, "Those aren't dandelions. Those are Wishing Flowers."

I stopped pulling and smiled.

2009 has been a challenge for many. But it's during challenging times, when we're reminded of how much we rely on our family and friends. So as we celebrate the birth of Jesus, we also celebrate the blessings He has given us; namely, that He has blessed us with all of you.

So from our family to yours: May 2010 be filled with fewer weeds and countless Wishing Flowers.

We love you,

The Posts

CHAPTER FOURTEEN
Christmas 2010

Preschool Christmas Play, Mudball & Bullies

Merry Christmas (Or Happy New Year - depending on when this letter arrives...),

A few days after we sent our last letter, Harper performed his "big" role in the preschool Christmas play. Since he's kind of shy in front of large (and small) groups, we were very surprised (and proud) that he was picked to be a shepherd.

Harper didn't have the lead role. That went to a motionless Cabbage Patch doll that played Jesus. Truthfully, when dealing with a preschool play, all the kids could lead, since you never truly know what they are going to say or do.

The play was cute. It started with a procession of all the "cast" - many of whom tripped or ran into the kid in front of them because they were scanning the audience and waving frantically to their parents instead of looking at where they were walking. The parents were waving back stiffly, because they didn't want to shake the camera that they were using to film their kid.

There was a glittery star hanging over a manger. Mary and Joseph made an appearance - surrounded by a frighteningly large amount of straw... There were two Wise Men - and one Wise Girl... There were two shepherds... There were various farm animals - including one boy dressed as a donkey crawling on his hands and knees who mooed loudly. (His mother in the audience gasped.)

Several girls dressed as angels were ringing bells in a dangerous flailing motion. One got clanked with the bell and her halo fell off. One kid galloped to the top of the risers, hopped off, and attempted a poorly executed somersault. (His father in the audience gasped.) Then two teachers (attempted to) gather all the rapscallions together to "direct" the chaos.

Some kids sang sweetly with their hands in prayer position. Some screamed the words to the song. Some kids screamed words that seemed to be from a different song. Some clapped without rhythm. Only one child cried and walked off stage to find his parents. In that confusion, one of the bell ringers found his "opening", escaped from the riser, grabbed the microphone and yelled, "Jesus!" (His grandmother gasped.)

And one cute little blonde scoundrel (with one eye closed and his head tilted) used his shepherd staff like a pool stick - as if the other shepherd's head was the cue ball. (My wife in the audience gasped.) At the end, everyone clapped - including all the kids… very energetically for themselves.

LESSONS FROM SPORTS

This past year kept the Post family engulfed in little people sports. A friend of mine once told me that all pee wee sports, whether soccer, basketball, football or t-ball, could be categorized as "Herd Ball."

Well, Harper was one of the little herders and, as discussed in last year's letter, he played basketball for the viciously intimidating Blue Splash Pops of Republic, Missouri. I am sad to report the year ended without a single victory. In fact, it ended with only 2 baskets made in all the games (Harper made none of those) and 5 shots made in all the practices (Harper made 3 of those). Harper's defense left a lot to be desired. It basically consisted of running alongside an opponent who was dribbling the ball, growling an angry face, then running past him under the hoop and throwing his body into the padded wall behind the basket. For his finale, he'd spin around in a few circles before returning to the court. Then, it was time to run to the other basket.

In our first game, there was lots of confusion and kids running into each other. In our last game, it looked a lot like our first game.

I could tell our Splash Pops were a little discouraged going into that last game. That was until the opposing team trotted onto the court. Upon looking at them, I thought these little kids had the wrong gym. They were TINY. Like two-year-old tiny. Up until that point, most of our opponents had large kids and you could tell before tip-off that it wasn't going to go well out there…But I just knew this game was going to be different.

The little blonde boy who "set their offense" was about 26 inches tall and had sports glasses. He had the most adorable little girls on his team with him. Their hair was in pigtails with matching pink polka-dotted ribbons. Their socks bunched around their ankles. Their little grey team t-shirts hung like dresses to their knees. One little girl during warm-ups carried the ball with both hands and nearly fell over from the weight of the ball. The ball was double her head circumference. Seriously.

I leaned over to Canton and said, "Finally, a team we can beat."

Canton smiled and nodded his head, and the two teams tipped off.

I can't tell you what happened next - because this letter is supposed to be family friendly. But there were moments when it looked like a prison riot. (Our team came out on the short end.) Not only did we not score, the gray little people scored eleven baskets - more than all of our other opponents combined.

After the game, Canton looked at me, patted my leg, and said, "I guess you learned your lesson here, huh, Dad?" I nodded emphatically.

MUD BALL - THE NEW SPORT

The volunteer coach for Harper's t-ball team was a nice man. ("Nice man" = slightly uncoordinated.) In addition, he had some odd quirks. For example, if it was partly cloudy outside, he would rather have practice in the gym than risk being rained on at the field. We got used to this as the season went on and adjusted our thought processes accordingly.

This was why we were stunned, when after a three-day monsoon, our coach called to tell us we'd be conducting practice outside. "It'll be fun," Coach said.

When we arrived at the field, I was in awe at the amount of no dirt there was. The field was a lake of MUD.

Now, my wife has been known to be slightly afraid of mud stains. But she has really getting into the supportive parent/athlete thing so she shrugged at me like, "Well, he's the coach. If he thinks it is okay..."

Coach was standing behind home plate. I am not exaggerating when I say that I could not see his shoes. That was how far into the mud he was lodged. I also noticed there were no other parents out there with their kids. Super.

He clapped and waved, "Hi guys. Get out there, and we'll hit a few grounders."

Harper couldn't stop staring at his footless coach.

I squished with Harper gingerly to the pitching mound.

Coach grabbed a bat and pointed at Harper. "Get ready, Harper, this one is coming to you."

Harper yelled, "OK!" and got into ready position with his knees bent and his glove in front of him.

Coach threw the ball into the air and (surprisingly) hit the ball in Harper's direction.

The ball splatted 10 feet in front of Harper and vanished into the mud. Harper looked up at me like he didn't know what to do (or that he was concerned that couldn't pry his feet from where he was standing).

I noticed his stress level and said, "I'll get it."

I trudged through the mud, scooped up the mud where the ball should have been, and was delighted that I actually found the ball. I held it out toward Harper, so he could throw it back to Coach. Harper squished up his nose like, "No thanks." So, I tried to throw it back to Coach. The ball weighed approximately 37 pounds with the mud on it, so it didn't quite make it to Coach. But as it wobbled through the air, mud clumps were flying off of it. That seemed to distract Coach who put up his hands to protect himself. This caused him to lose his balance and literally step right out of his shoes.

He looked down at his socks and said, "I don't need shoes today."

Harper told me he didn't need his shoes either and sat in the mud and took his cleats off. (Rana in the audience gasped.)

Hearing my wife's distress, I was about to yell at Harper to get his cleats back on, when I was hit unexpectedly in the back of the head by a hunk of mud.

I turned around and saw all three of our chubby outfielders (whose parents were sparkling clean in the bleachers) rolling in the mud and throwing clumps at each other. One chubby kid had mud smeared like war-paint on his evil face and was throwing clods at me. The parents were hollering for them to stop throwing mud and one even yelled, "You *don't* want me coming out there!"

169

I mumbled, "I do," and imagined pegging her with a mud glob. But I refrained, knowing I had to be a good example to Harper of good sportsmanship and positive attitude. Ah, the life of pee wee sports.

TROUBLE IN 2ND GRADE

I'm not talking about the trouble we parents have in deciphering our child's art projects when he brings home a funky, yellow, kiln-fired porcelain (misshapen) formation and asks us if we know what it is…

I'm not talking about the trouble that involved our son playfully slapping a girl's butt at recess because, and I quote: "Daddy does it to Mommy…"

I'm not talking about the trouble Daddy had trying not to pee on his own shoes when – at Back to School Night – Daddy had to use the little elementary urinal suspended only 12 inches off the ground.

And I'm not even talking about the confusion we experience in trying to remember if Friday is Wear-Pajamas Day, or if it is Wild-Hair-With-Inside-Out-Pajama Day, or if it is Wear-Your-Pajama-Bottoms- Inside-Out-and-Your-Sneakers-In-Your-Wild-Hair-Day…

And I'm not talking about grades either, because Canton is a star student…

I'm talking about knuckleheaded bullies.

Canton was having problems with one. I'm going to change his name to Melvin. Heck, I don't know why I'm changing his name since he ain't getting this letter.

Anyway, Canton told us about Melvin at dinner.

"He's always in trouble with the teachers… And he chases me and my friends around the playground. He trips us. He hits us and throws things at us!"

Rana was mortified. (This type of behavior should only happen on muddy baseball fields?)

"Uh, I have an idea," I said.

Everyone at the table looked at me. I felt self-conscious.

"Ask Melvin to play with you," I said.

I wish I had a picture of the bug-eyed stares I received at that moment. Especially from Canton and Rana. (Harper and the dog weren't really paying attention.)

Rana said, "I'm not sure getting closer to the punching boy is a good plan."

I said, "Maybe if he was asked to play, he wouldn't be punching."

After school on the next day, Canton hopped in the car. He literally leaned over the seat and gave me a choke-your-neck hug. He was grinning widely.

"Dad! Your plan worked like a charm," he clapped. "We asked Melvin to play with us and he looked surprised and then said, 'OK.'"

"Really?" I said. "Then what happened?"

"Nothing, we all just played together."

For the next two days it was more of the same. But, by the end of the week, Melvin was back to chasing Canton and basically every other kid in school. Melvin began throwing pinecones and other readily available objects such as pebbles and juice boxes. He was in trouble a lot and lost his recess privileges. But it was peaceful while it lasted.   And maybe Canton learned something, if only temporarily…

LANGUAGE BARRIER

As our kids get older, our toddler-talk deductive skills are wilting away.   We used to be able to decipher all forms of gobbledygook uttered from our toddler's mouth.   But our powers seem to have disappeared…

We were at a friend's house. Their spiky-haired 2 year old son ran up to me with a look of complete disbelief. He was holding out his plastic dinosaur from the movie Toy Story.

He shoved the toy in my face and screamed, "Miggie saury ist to do real ahhhhhh!"

I responded with the timeless classic, "Really?"

He didn't like that response. He screamed again, "Miggie saury ist to do real ahhhhhhhhh!"

I didn't know what to say, so I looked at my wife. She was always really good at this game when our kids were little. She looked at me and shrugged. Even Canton stared at me cluelessly.

Their child was now near tears. He really wanted me to help him. He shook the dinosaur in my face and yelled, "Miggie saury ist to do real ahhhhhhhhhhhhhhhhhhhhhhhhhhhhh!"

I was speechless. (As poorly evidenced by this 4 page letter.) But, for whatever reason, I was the one that this kid had latched onto for help.

My buddy's wife saved me from the kitchen: "He wants you to know his dinosaur has diarrhea!"

Oh.   Unfortunately, while my advice in thwarting school-yard bullies is rock solid, my expertise in stopping toy dinosaur diarrhea is questionable at best…

And though we don't hear the toddler babble much anymore, I am proud to tell you that Harper has started his own language. [If you are offended easily, please skip the next 8 lines.] You see, Harper has created a new word for...Well, the male parts.

It happened while we were wrestling. He accidentally kneed me in my (Christmas ornaments). I kind of grunted in pain and Harper laughed and said, "I hit you in the sackopedias!"

"My what?" I asked.

"Sackopedias are your balls!" he exclaimed.

"We don't call them balls," I said. "And where did you hear the word sackopedias?"

"Nowhere," Harper grinned proudly. "I just sayed it myself."

I don't know if the word will take off or not, but if you hear that it's being added to Webster's Dictionary, you'll know who started it...

Finally, as our children are getting older, they appear to be matching our wits more closely.

Example: The boys were at the table waiting to be fed. Rana and I were scrambling around the kitchen trying to throw together something for them to eat.

Harper: "I wanna' snack, please."

"Ok," I said.

Harper: "I wanna' snack please."

"I'm getting it," Rana said.

Harper laughed: "I wanna' snack please."

Rana: "If you say you want a snack one more time you are gonna' be in serious trouble, mister."

Harper: "Okay… Well, what happens to me if I say 'I want a drink, please?'"

***

I'll tie this letter up with this story:

Canton had a summer birthday. So, he had to invite kids to his party at the end of the school year. He only had a certain number of invitations. His instructions were clear: For the kids that we couldn't find addresses for, he must personally hand out the invitations. One week later, he still had one for Sydney. Rana told him that he must give the invitation to Sydney the next day, or she wasn't going to be able to come to the party. Canton agreed to "do his best" to get it to her.

At breakfast the next morning:

Rana: "What are you going to do at school today?"

Canton: "Give the invitation to Sydney or she's not coming to my party."

Rana and I gave an approving nod and smile…

While he was getting out of the car at school, I asked Canton, "What are you going to do today?"

He rolled his eyes and said, "Give the invitation to Sydney."

"Exactly," I said and kissed him goodbye…

Canton hopped in the car after school.

I immediately asked, "Did you give the invitation to Sydney?"

Canton nodded and said, "I took care of it."

174

"What does that *mean?*" I asked.

"I told her where my party was going to be and what time it was happening."

"Then what did you do with the invitation?" I asked.

"I gave it to Melvin," Canton said proudly.

"You gave it to *Melvin?!* Punching Melvin? The kid who hits you and your friends and is always in trouble?!? Why would you do that?"

"You told me to be nice to him," Canton replied.

When we got home, Rana met us at the door. We hadn't closed the door when she asked, "Did you give Sydney her invitation?"

Canton said, "I told dad I took care of it."

Rana, "What does 'I took care of it' mean?"

Me: "He gave the invitation to Melvin."

Rana: "Melvin?!? The kid who is always mean and hitting everyone? That's who you invited to your party? We're responsible when he's at your party! What if he hits other kids - or us?!?"

Canton nodded and reminded her that I had told him to try being nice to Melvin.

Rana - who earlier was moved that my advice had gone off so well - was now looking at me like I was not smart.

"Well, what's done is done," Rana said, throwing up her hands.

I arrived at school the next day and opened my e-mail. I quickly noticed an e-mail from Melvin's mom. The subject line was: "YOUR SON." Yep - in all capital letters. Gulp.

I opened the email ready to discipline Canton. It read: "You may not know me, but I work at your son's school. I have watched Canton the last few years when he interacts with my son and I have to tell you that he is the kindest, most patient little boy I have ever been around. Melvin can be difficult. He looks normal, but he has severe emotional and developmental issues.

That being said, we can't tell you how much it meant to Melvin that Canton invited him to his birthday party. I can count on one hand how many birthday parties Melvin's ever been invited to and he was so excited to tell me he had been invited to Canton's party that he could hardly contain himself. We won't be able to come to his party, as we will be on vacation, but just wanted to let you know what an amazing little boy you have."

I forwarded the email to my wife, who replied with, "I can't type right now because I'm crying."

I tell this story not looking for a parental pat on the back, but to show that sometimes, just being nice to someone is what they might have needed all along. So, during this season of hustle and bustle, traffic, crowds, and travel, I hope each of us can embrace others with the heart of a 2nd grader.

God's blessings to you and yours during this holiday season and the year ahead.

Love always,

John, Rana, Mud-baller Harper, Bully-Whisperer Canton, and Montana

CHAPTER FIFTEEN
Christmas 2011

*Disney World & Karate
(Not Necessarily Combined)*

Dear Friends,

It was November 26th at 12:15 AM. I was driving - my wife and kids were cashed out. I had just navigated the curvy, dark roads of Arkansas and entered the lively town of Thayer, Missouri. It was there that it happened. Our car was attacked by an enormous pair of Mickey Mouse ears. Terrifying hallucinations of this kind are common after you've driven 17 straight hours home from Disney World. (The thought that the ears were trying to pull another dollar out of my wallet only added to my horror.) My gasp of panic did not awaken my wife. So I elbowed her.

"I'm glad you're resting so peacefully, but I'm dyin' here," I said. "You gotta' talk to me. Ask me a question or something."

Rana rubbed her eyes and thought for a second. "Have you started the Christmas letter yet?"

Well, that was an excellent question, because I had not started the letter yet. But it got my mind racing. What was I going to put in the Christmas letter this year? More importantly, after Disney World, could we afford to buy stamps to send out the Christmas letter? So many questions that kept us awake until we pulled safely into our driveway and collapsed.

I decided to start this letter with Disney World because the trip was so amazing. (By amazing, I mean expensive.) We went on this trip with our wonderful friends, the Goughs. (By wonderful, I really mean wonderful.)

Now, I know I try to keep these Christmas letters funny. But, the truth is, there is absolutely nothing funny about Disney World. It's often called, "The Happiest Place on Earth." I don't know who named it that, but that person must have been drinking heavily. The truth of the matter is that Disney World should be called, "Where Emotionally Spent Parents Drag Their Crying Kids."

The irritation starts at the front gate - where the overly-friendly, airport-like security guy goes through your bag and makes comments about the large quantity of snacks and drinks you're trying to smuggle into the park.

Once in the park, the tension increases. Parents are vigorously pulling their kids along to as many rides as humanly possible and forcing them to take pictures with monster-sized Poohs, dangerously large depressed donkeys, enormous ducks with speech impediments, etc. (Side note: Forcing your child to take a picture with an oversized Pooh is wrong on so many levels.) All this time, the children are resisting their parents and yanking them in the opposite direction toward the Disney food carts and souvenir stores.

For demonstration purposes, here are the **Top Ten** quotes we heard most often at Disney World:

1) *"How* much!?!"

2) *"Another* souvenir store?!"

3) "Is that *the line?"*

4) "Stop crying." (This is said by adults to their children and by adults to their spouses.)

5) "I need to go to the bathroom!"

6) "You *just* went to the bathroom!"

7) "I'm hungry."

8) "I can't afford to feed you here."

9) "Where the hell did we park?"

10) "Why didn't *I* come up with this Disney World idea?"

And the joy keeps flowing – even as the parents are heading out of the park – carrying their sack-of-potato children over their shoulders.

Mother: "Can you walk a little faster? We'll never make the tram!"

Father: "I could walk faster if I wasn't carrying these heavy-ass kids – that must have gained 50 pounds each from inhaling the snacks you packed today!"

Mother: "Shut up and walk."

Father mumbling: "I wish you had fallen off Space Mountain…"

The only Disney park where the adults seem genuinely happy is at Epcot. (I believe that is where the "Happiest Place on Earth" slogan was created.) The reason for that is Epcot offers a plethora of alcoholic beverages from countries around the world. You can get Saki in Japan, beer in Germany, and margaritas in Mexico. The ladies working in France making the Grand Marnier martinis seemed to generate the most smiles for a number of reasons.

While everyone else at the park seemed to be miserable, the Posts and Goughs had a blast. We laughed and frolicked through the parks without a care in the world. Our kids smiled, were patient with the 1400 pictures we took, and "ooh'ed" and "aaw'ed" as we soaked in the nightly fireworks shows and daily the Florida sun. We will never forget our trip to Disney World. It really was magical…

***

This year, the Post family was still immersed in the wild world of sports (and probably will be for years to come). We obviously love following Mizzou football and basketball, but the boys participated in their own individual sports, too. Harper played t-ball again and Canton was in swimming. But they agreed to take "fitness" karate together. When we approached them about it, Canton asked if he'd be breaking wood boards with his hands – and

181

if he was, he wasn't interested. Harper said he'd ONLY be interested if he would be breaking wood boards with his hands.

The room where the karate class took place was a long rectangle with a whiteboard running along the entire front of it. The class started with each child drawing a "bad guy" on the board in front of them with an Expo marker. The kids would eventually "fight" their bad guys. Harper drew what looked like a possessed green taco – or maybe it was a Disney character – I couldn't be sure. Another girl spent about 10 minutes drawing a blue jack-o-lantern with huge bunny ears. The instructor was waiting (not patiently).

The spiky, gray-haired instructor's name was Polly. She was a spunky 60 year old and was only about 4 inches taller than Harper. But we didn't let the age and height fool us. What she "lacked" in those categories, she more than made up for with the oak trees she possessed for thighs. Mercy. Anyway, Polly was ready to begin class. She tightened the knot of the black belt around her waist and bowed.

One boy hopped/skipped into the room late and Polly said gruffly, "We don't have time for you to draw a bad guy, so I'll do it." She proceeded to draw a circle with two dots for eyes. The boy didn't think his bad guy looked very scary. Polly then scribbled a zigzag line for the mouth and the boy smiled.

The class finally began. All the kids stood in front of their "bad guy" and bowed. Polly told the kids the five training principles for karate. Then, she made the mistake of asking them to repeat the principles.

One boy blurted out, "Be respectful, be brave, and get lots of presents from Santa." All the kids howled in laughter. Polly said, "Well, I said *five* principles and you gave me *three*." Canton raised his hand and completed the list. Polly sort-of smiled. She then moved on to stretching by touching her forehead to the floor....The bunny ear girl fell over.

Polly continued to stretch at hyper speed. She was yelling out, "Lunge left!" and "Switch to the right, bend your right knee!" – and the kid who couldn't count obviously didn't know his right from left either because he was gyrating his bent limbs back and forth like a wounded horse. But he wasn't alone – most of the kids were flailing their arms and bent knees in a frightening manner. Harper turned to us as if to say, "There is nothing about this that resembles breaking wood with my hands."

Then the punching began. The kids yelled, "Keee-ya!" every time they threw a punch. Polly was showing them how to punch straight in front of them – as if they were punching someone in the stomach. Then each kid approached her and "punched" at a red, padded square she had velcroed to her hand. Kids were screaming, "Keee-ya!" even when they were just standing in line waiting to punch Polly. Harper's first punch looked not like a punch – but an overhand clubbing motion. She corrected this behavior by popping Harper in the top of his head with the red punching pad. She said, "You punch like that and you're gonna' get your nose bloodied." Harper turned to us and smiled. Canton turned to us and looked horrified.

A cute, little girl with a blonde pony-tail came up and smiled at Polly. The instructor popped her in the top of her head with the square. "Little Miss, you are so sweet. But sweet is going to get you beat up. When you walk up here, you have to have your fists up and ready." The girl nodded and yelled "Keee-ya" as she ran to the back of the line.

The highlight of the class was when the children began to practice kicks with Polly. She was not impressed with their lack of balance or flexibility. Most of the kid's kicking motion resembled that of kicking a rock down the street. Polly was yelling, "No, no, no! That won't injure anyone you are attacking. Kick to the head or chest!" She was grabbing kid's feet and pulling them toward the sky so they understood the correct attack position. Kids were falling all over themselves. The kid who made the Santa joke? Well, his foot got a little extra tug from Polly. I think it was the only time she chuckled.

While sports (and Polly) didn't kill us, we did experience our first "family" death this year. (You can't pay for transitions like the one I just did there.) It was Harper's fish and he had been swimming happily in his aquarium for two years.

Rana called me into his bedroom and pointed to the fish breathing heavily on the bottom of the tank. He was kind of sideways. The boys asked me to leave him in the aquarium for just a few minutes longer, so they could draw a picture to remember him. They both gathered around the aquarium with their markers and drew the upside down fish. (Canton reminded Harper that the fish's eyes should be X's and not dots.)

I got a net, pulled him out of the aquarium, and we had a funeral procession to the bathroom. Before I flushed, we all stared into the toilet and waved goodbye to him. Canton said, "We'll see you in heaven."

The boys were crying. Rana and I were crying. So we decided we should go to bed and say our prayers. Both boys had their eyes clenched shut and their fingers locked together in prayer position.

Canton: "Dear Lord, thank you for Harper's fishes' life. He was a good fish. We hope to see him again… We really loved, uh…" He opened his eyes, looked at Harper and asked, "What was his name again?"

Harper was kind of startled and his eyes flew open. He unclenched his fingers. He paused for a long moment, and with a puzzled expression said," Uh…Uh… I think his name was Pinky."

Canton nodded: "Okay. We will miss you, ole' Pinky. Amen."

Rana and I had to turn our heads to hide our grins at Harper naming his fish post-mortem.

Speaking of old (you'll appreciate this brilliant transition too; just keep reading)....This year, our family had really gotten into watching the show "American Pickers" about two guys who travel the country and buy antiques from old farm houses to resell in their store. Well, our boys have really bought into the idea that old things can be special and valuable. Just because it's old, doesn't mean its trash. We've tried to help them appreciate vintage items as much as their new, cooler, more modern gadgets. The questions began to abound in our house: "Harper, is this bottle cap rare?" or "Is this old Big Bird puzzle worth anything?" They were really building an appreciation for items of yesteryear.

We started going to local antique shops and flea markets so the kids could look around. They took such delight in finding old Matchbox cars or Sesame Street games for a bargain. (When they found a treasure, I liken their giddy grins to someone who may have partaken of Das Beergarten at Epcot.)

Rana and I also found some treasures: vintage pictures, old Mizzou drinking glasses, etc. One day on the counter by the cash register, I found some local home-made jars of strawberry jam. They looked delicious. I told the boys I'd share it with them and use it for a special PB and J in their school lunches.

The next day, when I was cleaning out Canton' lunchbox, I noticed he hadn't eaten his sandwich which I had made with this special jam.

I called him into the kitchen.

Me: "Canton, are you feeling okay? You didn't eat your sandwich today."

Canton wrinkled his brow and appeared to have tears welling in his eyes. He said, "Dad I can't believe you'd try to force me to eat that old, antique jelly!"

School for both boys has been going well. Canton was elected to Student Council and he really has been loving saying the morning announcements over the intercom. According to his teachers, Canton has a very peppy "game show host" voice he pulls out of his back of tricks. He also had a speaking part in his 4th grade Christmas play.

Rana recently asked Harper if he wanted to be in Student Council like his brother when he got into the 4th grade. Harper replied, "I don't need that kind of responsibility."

That makes sense because Harper is so busy right now in the big, bad world of kindergarten. And this year has been a little more challenging for him. Childhood development experts (Rana included) say that firstborns take charge, and the youngest children are "all about fun." As I type this, Canton is reading a book for his reading log and Harper is trying to roll under our dog's legs.

This is kind of symbolic of how Harper's year started off. One day he came home proudly announcing he had gotten into some trouble. This did not go over very well with me. I sternly asked him what he did and he said that several boys in the class made him laugh and the teacher told him if he didn't calm down, he'd have to sit in the Safety Seat. (I actually thought the Safety Seat sounded like a positive thing – but Harper said it was for bad kids only. I really think they need to rename the Safety Seat to the "Sucky Seat" so parents know it is a punishment sort of deal.)

Anyway, I told Harper he better be good the next day. He nodded – in an irritated way. (There may have been an eye-roll.)

186

The next day, I got an email at work that said Harper had put a lima bean so far up another student's nose that the school nurse had to remove it. I thought my head was going to explode. When I picked him up, I asked him what in the world he was thinking.

Harper: "Jyger told me to shove it in there because he said it would be funny."

Me: "I told you to stop goofing off with your friends!"

Harper: "That's it! I'm done with friends. They are nothing but trouble. I will tell them tomorrow that I don't want any of them anymore!"

I kind of chuckled (in an irritated way) and explained that friends were great but there was a time to laugh and have fun, and there was a time to listen to the teacher. He seemed to get it, and since then, has been a stellar student. He even got an academic award at a recent assembly. And, I am proud to report that he still has friends...quite a few of them, actually.

Rana, however, has not been liking the "friends" she's been stuck with in her MBA Healthcare Administration graduate classes. See, Rana's a very good student who meets deadlines. However, she recently pondered implanting lima beans (or larger legumes) into her classmates' noses since several of those group members seemed to love saving group project duties until the last minute – or not finishing them at all. She keeps telling herself, "Only seventeen more months to go!"

Ok, I'll tie this up, since my wife needs the computer to write a paper for her class now...

Harper came home from school one day and said, "A boy was mean and stuck his tongue out at me today at recess."

I opened my mouth to save the day and Canton stopped me. "I took care of this already, Dad."

Harper nodded and said, "Yeah, brother took care of it."

Me: "You didn't Polly karate kick him did you?"

Both boys just stared at my dumbness.

Rana: "Canton, how did you take care of it?"

Canton: "Harper told me about this at lunch so I said, 'When you see that mean boy, tell him that Martin Luther King taught peace and sticking out your tongue isn't peaceful…then what would he say to that? Nothing.'"

Harper, still nodding: "I told that mean boy exactly what Canton said."

Me: "Well, what did the mean boy say when you said that?"

Harper: "He said sorry and put his arm around me."

That story made us smile. And maybe gave us a little something to think about. During this upcoming year, when it feels like life is sticking its tongue out at us – head to Epcot. (Just kidding.)

We pray that in 2012, God grants all of us a little extra peace in our hearts and provides us the grace and strength to deal with whatever comes our way…

We love you,

The Four Postketeers

CHAPTER SIXTEEN
Christmas 2012

*Know-It-Alls, School Projects
& Flag Football*

Dear Everyone (who is reading this letter),

Last year, we were spending December recovering from our magical trip to Disney World. This year we've been spending December recovering from having an 11 and a 7-year-old running our house. School, sports, refereeing rough-housing, and preventing two boys from constantly saying, "I'm sooooo hungry!" seem to take up the majority of our time.

Our boys *do* love to rough house. A lot. So far, we have averted a visit to the emergency room. But a few days ago, upon looking outside and seeing the boys wrestling like twisted pretzels on the grass (but moving ever-closer to the street), all the while trying to pry themselves apart with one of my golf clubs, I had seen enough.

Me: Boys! Find another game to play that doesn't involve the pavement or whapping each other with sporting equipment! Got it?

Harper: Fine…But can we at least still dominate the universe?!

Me: Uh, I guess so.

Harper started first grade this year and is thriving. By thriving, I mean he is pretty sure he's Albert Einstein's son (and that isn't remotely close to being true). Here's an example:

Rana and Harper were studying for his spelling test. He hadn't missed a word yet. But he seemed to want to practice one word in particular – over and over again.

Rana: Ok, you just spelled it correctly a second ago…But we'll do it again. How do you spell "but"?

Harper: B-U-T. Just one "t" because the other "t" would make "butt" – like this thing right here… (He pointed to his rump and burst into hysterical, knee-slapping laughter.)

Rana looked at me as if to indicate that if she had to listen to him spell that word one more time, and she had to hear that joke

191

one more time, and I stood there motionless and let it happen one more time…We may get divorced.

Rana: You know, Harp, you can also ask Daddy anything for your class too. He teaches Language Arts and knows a lot.

I nodded with a lot of gusto so he (and she) could see me.

Harper: Ok… Well, I know he teaches Language Arts, but does he know *sign* language?

Rana: Daddy, do you know sign language?

Me: Uh, no.

Harper: Well then, you doesn't know as much as me, because I know how to sign the word for "bathroom."

Rana: Oh… Well then, okay, spell "but" for me one more time….The kind with one "t."

Harper's teacher confirmed that not only can he spell well, but at his parent teacher conference, she showed us samples of his writing. She said that Harper had more topic ideas for his essays than any other kid in class. She showed us a few from his notebook:

- "What would happen if the students knew more than the teacher?" (Good idea…Funny and witty – with a dash of confidence. I like that.)

- "What would happen if a student broke the teacher's computer?" (Nice…An essay with a hint of danger and suspense. I'd read it.)

- "What would happen if daddy didn't yell the bad "S" word at the Mizzou game?" (If you would have seen Mizzou play that night, you would have described it with the bad "S" word too…And maybe more than once.)

Rana just stared at me. Harper's teacher just smiled.

This year, Canton entered the 5th grade. For those keeping track at home, 5th grade is officially the beginning of intermediate school in our school district. The term "Intermediate school" seems to give off the impression that there is a transition going on within your child. That would be incorrect. You see, intermediate school should be called immediate school. I say this because as soon as your child enters it, they immediately acquire an adult-sized attitude accompanied by variations of the following conversation at least once a week:

Me: Boys, it's time for bed.

Canton enters the room: Hey Dad?

Me: Yeah?

Canton: Dad, we're doing "this thing" in Social Studies. (For the record, "this thing" is a very popular phrase uttered by intermediate school kids. Loosely translated it means: big-ass project.)

Me: Okay, what do you need?

Canton: Well, we just need a few things. (For intermediate school people, the words "a few" is often confused with the words, "a ton of." Also, notice the word "we" is used incorrectly. The pronoun should be "I".)

Me: Okay, what things do you need?

Canton: Well... I just need a railroad train set, a Martin Luther King Jr. medallion, three full size logs, a block of dry ice, a fake Mt. Vesuvius volcano, one Krispy Kreme doughnut, and ten jars of artichoke marmalade. And some glue - the kind that NASA uses to hold together bolts on the Space Shuttle.

Me: [No words... I'm just staring at him.]

Canton: And...We need those by tomorrow.

Me (in my head): Bad "S" word, bad "S" word, bad "S" word.

We were surprised that while Canton had enough wherewithal to run a Student Council Movie Night, host a pizza fundraiser event including ticket sales, and be the emcee for the school talent show, he still couldn't manage to pick up his room after five reminders. I know this because Rana was recently helping him with this task when, from under his bed, she dug out a Portuguese water dogs calendar. It was cute... and from the year 2009.

Have you ever seen the movie *Four Weddings and a Funeral*? I haven't because I heard it was average at best, but I couldn't think of another transition here. You see, we've been to almost four weddings this year and one funeral. I guess those numbers are ok – and significantly better than one wedding and four funerals.

The summer weddings are particularly inconvenient for me because I am hot-natured...Dress clothes make me sweat even more... So, we were sardined in a cram-packed pew waiting for this sweltering wedding to begin. I was fanning myself with a hymnal book. (Does God mind that?) The processional music started playing and I mumbled, "Thank God."

Harper looked at me and asked, "Thank God, for what?"

I said, "Uh, thank God this beautiful wedding is starting."

Harper nodded and smiled.

This event was kind of exciting for Harper because it was the first wedding he had attended since he was an infant – so the whole experience was "new" to him. The music started playing and Harper was craning his neck to see. Suddenly, his eyes bulged as he watched the whole wedding party stepping slowly down the aisle – from ring bearers, to flower throwers, to groomsmen, to bridesmaids...

Harper leaned over to me and asked, "Are all these people getting married today?!"

"No," I said.

He replied, "Oh good. This wedding would have taken *forever!*"

After the wedding was over, the boys devoured much cake. (In my opinion, free cake is the best part of any wedding – especially since our boys are always hungry.) As we all enjoyed the cake, Rana asked Harper if he liked the wedding. He said, "Nah. It was like church, but with too much kissing."

Canton, on the other hand, said he liked the wedding a lot. And , for the first time, he said he didn't mind the kissing. And so it begins! I should have been alerted to Canton's shift in philosophy when over- hearing a recent conversation between Canton and Harper on the drive home from school:

Canton: You got a girlfriend yet?

Harper furrowed his brow: No way!

Canton: Well, you're never going to be happily married if you don't find yourself a girlfriend.

We aren't too worried because we think Harper will end up with some girl who will appreciate his athletic prowess. See, Harper is fast. He used this skill to play flag football this fall. He was the only kid on the team who scored: 8 touchdowns in 5 games. The season was 6 games total, but the first game consisted of Harper running straight up the middle into a "child" that looked like he might have driven himself to the game.

On the car ride home after the game, Rana went Vince Lombardi on Harper:

(Coach) Rana: Why would you run *right* into the boys in front of you?

Harper: I don't know?

Rana: Well, I have an idea. Instead of running straight into the pile of kids every time (she was relying on her football knowledge that I had bestowed on her early in our marriage), you could use your speed to run *around* them.

Harper: [No words...he was just staring.]

Before the next game's kickoff, Rana reminded Harper that "around" NOT "into" was the name of the plan. Harper actually took Rana's advice and scored 2 times.

After the game, Rana asked, "How did you run that fast?"

Harper said matter-of-factly, "Well, I just pretended that mean, angry dogs were chasing me."

While offense was his specialty, Harper was a little less interested in playing solid defense. While he had no problem catching up to kids who were carrying the ball, his strategy was to run alongside of them with a mean, angry face and "fake" like he was going to grab their flag. Sounds a little like pee wee basketball of yesteryear, doesn't it? While surely intimidating, no opponent with the ball stopped running due to fear or dropped the ball in terror. So, we assume that while Harper could pretend mean, angry dogs were chasing him when he had the ball, he couldn't translate that into becoming the mean, angry dog himself.

Fair enough.

Well, I feel carpal tunnel coming on - which means it is time to tie this up...

I mentioned earlier that we had a funeral of sorts. This summer we had to put our yellow lab mix, Montana, to sleep.

Twelve wonderful years… As the vet told me, "He was your first baby boy." (Wow – Doc, thanks! I wasn't sobbing enough as it was.)

The house doesn't feel the same without Montana's sweet face peeking out at us behind the couch… But we know he is racing around the fields of Heaven with strong legs like he had when he was younger, and that thought makes us smile…

As I pull my eyes away from my laptop and look at our mantel, I notice Montana's red paw stocking is missing. Losing him has deeply impacted us in ways we never imagined it would. We have always appreciated our family time together, but it seems that now, we soak in the joyous raucous sounds of boys rough-housing induced laughter with a patient grin instead of an immediate reprimand…We make sure we tell the boys how proud we are of them and how much we love them…And I've noticed that when we hug them –we let those hugs linger just a little longer.

In 2013, may God grant each of you, health – and countless opportunities to enjoy the warmth and love of your families and friends. We are so thankful for each of you.

All our Love (and an extra-long hug),

John, Rana, Canton, Harper, and Jesus's
right hand dog, Montana

198

CHAPTER SEVENTEEN
Christmas 2013

THE Sex Talk, Reconciliation, Sports & a New Puppy

200

D

ear Loved Ones,

I know this is supposed to be a "family-friendly" publication, but this letter is going to start off with a bang. (You'll get the brilliance of this lead-in momentarily.)

Canton came home from school and told Rana that he overheard two boys discussing some "weird things." He described those things in more detail, and Rana called me into the kitchen (urgently).

Rana: "Canton needs to talk to you."

Me: "Ok, what about?"

Rana: "*Things.*"

Me: "I'm bad at this game."

Rana: "*Thingggsssss,*" and she gave me an eyebrow-raising, Groucho Marx look.

(Gulp.) I led Canton into our bedroom. As we walked, I tried to mentally prepare myself for questions – that even as a 40 year old man - I may still have trouble answering... Canton got up on our bed and I sat next down to him. He looked vaguely (very) uncomfortable.

Me: (I took a deep breath.) "Ok, what questions do you have? You can ask me *anything.*"

Canton: "Ok…Dad, what do you know about sex?"

Me: (At this point I imagined a bomb defuser trying to decide which wire to cut first. Cut the wrong one, and "KABOOM!" After a few seconds, I came up with the following gem:) "Well, son, let me just say that you came to the right…Err, I know A LOT about… Uh, what *exactly* do you want to know?"

201

Canton: "Ok, what *exactly* is sex? Like, how does it all work?"

Me: "Uh, good starting question…Well, when a man loves a woman…" (No, I didn't sing it, but I did chuckle a bit when the words came out.)

Canton: "Dad, be serious."

Me: "Sorry." So I cleared my throat and explained sex. I was pretty proud of my word choice. I believe I even used some accurate, yet tactful, hand gestures.

Canton was staring at me like he accidentally ate a vegetable. But I could tell he wanted to ask me something else.

Me: "Go ahead, bud. Ask me anything."

Canton: "Do you and mom have sex?"

Me: "Uh….Yes. How do you think you and Harper got here?"

Canton: "So you and mom have only had sex *two times?*"

Me: "Uh, not exactly…"

Canton: "Well, how many more times than twice have you guys done it?"

Me: "Uh, I haven't really counted."

Canton: "So, like, do you do it *a lot?*"

Me: "Well, we do it…Hmmmm…All the….Err, I mean…..Every…..Uh, I mean….Once a….Uhhh….."

Canton: "Dad, that's plain weird."

There was an awkward silence.

Canton: "Ok, Dad, I have to ask…*Where* do you and mom do it?"

Me: "Ummmmm…" (I can't keep my eyes from looking down at the bed we're sitting on.)

Canton followed my eyes and nearly jumped off the bed. Then he yelled: "You do it *here*???!!!!!!"

Me: "Well, not exclusively, we also…Never mind…Yes, we *only* do it here."

Canton: "Do you at least *close the door*?"

Me: "Of course."

Canton: "So every time the door is closed and you guys are in here, you're *having sex*?!"

Me: (I actually had to pause to think about that.) "No."

Canton: (His eyes suddenly flew open wide.) "Wait a minute! That time the door was closed and I opened it and asked what you were doing and you said you and mom were just wrestling….You were really *having sex*??!!!!"

Me: "Uh…Yes... But we learned a valuable lesson about locking doors."

Canton: OK, Dad, thanks for explaining sex to me. I feel a lot *better*? (He actually inflected the word "better" with a question mark.)

Moving on to a much needed spiritual note… Harper will be receiving his first Communion in 2014. In order for Harper to prepare, his church class participated in the following activity leading up to his first Reconcilation: The children and their parents read a list of about 267 common sins. The children were then asked to take a pebble from a bucket and place it temporarily inside their shoe for every sin they (admitted) committing from the list. This was to show how sins "hurt" us and God as we "carry" them around…The kid next to Harper had apparently had a pretty rough year. I know this because he dropped so many pebbles in his shoe, he couldn't get his shoe back on his foot. But, you will be happy to know that Harper only placed 3 pebbles in his own shoe – all revolving around not showing "brotherly love."

Anyway, the highlight of the event came at this pebble dispersing moment:

Rana: "…#195 on the list is 'cheats on tests at school.'"

Harper: "No way."

Rana: "…#196 is 'steals things that don't belong to you.'"

Harper: "Nope."

Rana: "…#197 is 'talks about others or gossips.'"

Harper: "No… But, Mom, *you* better get one of those pebbles."

Rana: "What? Hey, this isn't about me."

Harper: "Ok. Then you might as well get some pebbles for Dad because he says bad words when he watches Mizzou on TV. (I will say, our son might be somewhat clairvoyant – since, when watching Mizzou lose the SEC Championship game, I needed one… dump truck load.)

But honestly, I'm not sure Harper is the one who should be throwing stones here (now, that was pretty clever) based upon this recent transgression:

Canton: "Dad! Harper said I should bend over so he could kick me in my 'a!'"

Rana: "Harper? You said the bad 'a' word?"

Harper: "Oh, just *delightful*, Canton! Now, I'm going to need *another* pebble!"

Even though Harper played baseball, football, and basketball this year for the Republic Sharks (ironically, we said no to water polo because his swimming skills are questionable), I am certain that Harper didn't learn the 'a' word from his coach. I know Coach Mike is *very* careful not to use the 'a' word. He's way too refined to use such barbaric language. Instead, he hollers things like, "Boys, you better get your **donkeys** moving!"

I laugh every time I hear that – no matter the sport. But, generally, sports are no laughing matter – unless of course you recall that Harper used to play for the viciously intimidating Blue Splash Pops. Now, that name *was* a laughing matter. Well, that was kindergarten. This is 2nd grade Sharks basketball and it is *serious* business. And it's mostly the parent spectators who make it that way.

I've noticed that when second graders shoot (see: blindly launch) the basketball in the direction of the rim, every parent in the crowd leans and lurches their bodies hoping to aid the ball into the hoop. Our own emphatic gyration hasn't worked much for Harper's team as the Sharks have only made 9 shots...in 10 games. (On the bright side, if intentional fouling, double dribbling, or standing stationary while watching the other teams shoot and rebound, earned you points, we'd be undefeated.)

Related sports side-note: Canton had a few boys in his class last year who weren't very nice to him. He asked what I thought he should do. We talked about how team sports had really helped Harper establish a solid peer group. But every kid is different. Harper is more the, "I-like-to-throw-myself-on-the-ground-and-get-dirty" kind of kid. Canton is more the "I'd-like-to-stay-upright-and-clean" kind of kid. So I had a terrific solution to help him with the mean boys: I proposed Canton take up golf. After all, most golfers don't end up on the ground.

Me: I think you should play an organized sport. What about…golf?"

Canton: "These boys are mean, Dad. How would playing golf help me with that?"

Me: "Well, when you're part of a team –"

Canton interrupts: "Oh, wait! I get it! The golf team will teach me how to whack those boys really hard with my golf club?!"

Me: "That's not exactly what – "

Harper interrupts: "Ooooh!!! Could I play golf?!!"

It's not like Canton really needs my help, I guess. I mean, he is *very* involved in school. He runs three miles every Wednesday with the school's Running Club. He was also nominated for Peer Ambassadors in 6th grade – which means he helps do "interventions" with students who have disagreements. He mediates and helps them discover acceptable solutions for their problems. He is even able to offer helpful advice. This job is perfect for Canton because he is right 100% of the time. Plus, he understands what "confidentiality" means. He proved this when I asked him how his first intervention went and he told me, "Dad, I'm sorry, but I'm not allowed to discuss the details of the meetings." (That's interesting, because he sings like a jailbird when his brother offers to kick his donkey.)

With the boys' activities pulling us in many directions, I needed to reconsider my coaching duties at the middle school. But I wasn't totally sure I was ready to let go of coaching – I had embraced this part of my job for the past 14 years. That changed on the night of September 16th.

A little background: Because I coached middle school football for 8 years, Coach Mike deemed me skilled enough to be the Shark's flag football offensive coordinator this year. (His only piece of advice when calling plays: "Please give Harper the ball." I told him that I'd try to show a little more variety than that.)

The first two games, I was in the huddle calling the plays, and Harper was a little touchdown making machine. (I swear I had other kids carrying the ball too.) Well, we won both games. On the date of the third game, I had to coach at a cross country meet and couldn't be with Harper in the huddle.

At about 7:30, Rana called me as I was on the bus headed home to tell me Harper's team lost. I was surprised by this. She then told me Harper "wasn't his normal self" during the game, and that he needed to talk to me. She handed him the phone.

Harper (with tears in his voice): "Daddy, *where* are you?"

Me: "Remember, bud? I had a cross country meet tonight."

Harper (more tears): "But Daddy, I *needed* you."

Me: (some tears of my own): "I'm so sorry, bud."

Harper: "It's okay."

But I knew it *wasn't* okay... The next morning, I turned in my coaching resignation – effective at the end of this cross country season. It was time to focus on "coaching" **my own** kids. (And, boy did I get to coach... Harper's team won their last 3 football games – including beating the defending champion who had never lost a game in two years. In that game, Harper raced for 5 touchdowns. The Republic Sharks finished as the league champion and Harper was all smiles with his daddy by his side.☺)

Letting go of middle school coaching has provided several positives. For one, I won't have to hear 7th grade cross country runners at practice ask, "Do we have to *run* today?" Additionally, it will free me up for not only Canton and Harper, but for Rana, who, may potentially be making a career change.

207

See, Rana completed her MBA this past October. It took 2 ½ years and cost approximately $1.4 million dollars. There were moments when she thought she might not get through – what with many of her group classmates doing little to contribute. But she finished – with straight A's actually. We are all very proud of her. We trust God will place her where she needs to be.

Well, as this is probably the longest Christmas letter you will receive this year, I promise that it is almost over…

This past year we had an unexpected addition to our family. (This has *nothing* to do with the conversation I had with Canton at the beginning of this letter.) You might remember that last summer we had to put our Lab, Montana, to sleep after 12 wonderful years with our family. We vowed never to get another dog, because losing him was so hard. Plus, you may recall our (my) disasterous choice when we almost adopted that devil dog, Truman…

Well, this July, a little, female, floppy-eared dog squeezed under our fence. I knew I was in trouble as soon as the boys and Rana laid eyes on her face. (Harper tells people she's a "Dachshund and 'Bugle' mix." She is apparently quite *musical?*) Anyway, when she showed up, she was in rough shape – obviously abandoned, malnourished, and covered with ticks/fleas. We checked with several neighbors to see where she might belong. No one claimed her. (Dang it.)

Then, came the dinner conversation:

Harper, Canton, (and Rana): "You *can't* let her die, Dad. We *have* to help her. She *needs* us."

That night they named her Annabelle. (My vote was "Annabeast" after she chewed up one of my sandals.)

My mom says that Montana sent Annabelle to us to fill our broken hearts. Mom is probably right about that…

Anyway, when we brought Annabelle to our vet to get her on the path back to health, we told him about how she *just showed up*… He smiled and said, "You know, the *best* ones find *you.*"

And, as we sit down and reflect on last year – in a sense, that quote really applies to all of you. How blessed we are that you have found us along the way. Our lives are rich with joy, because of the love you give us. Our lives are full and beautiful because of you.

May God bless you this holiday season, next year, and beyond.

We love you,

Canton, Harper, John, Rana (Beauty), and Annabelle (the Beast)

CHAPTER EIGHTEEN

Christmas 2014

A Teenager Has Invaded our Home & Manners at Church

Greetings from Missouri (unless you're getting this letter and you already reside in Missouri, in which case I mean, "Greetings from Where You Currently Live"),

So I'm sitting here typing this letter from home at 7:14 on a Wednesday morning because we've got two sick boys at home. Harper summed up all our sentiments last night before bed when he said, "I sure hope I don't get *The Nauseous.*" I agreed completely. That sounded very serious (and messy).

Any way… Last year, I started off the Christmas letter "with a bang" by describing The S-E-X talk I had with Canton. This year, I will begin with a related story. (I just want to keep it consistent. This is not necessarily an indication of where my mind has been residing the majority of the year.)

Harper is only in 3rd grade and, thankfully, he's not at all ready for "*The* Talk." However, he had a moment of insight recently that I will likely revisit when the time comes:

We were driving on a winding country road when we saw two horses in a field. (I promise the story gets better.) Typically when we see horses, they are out in the middle of the field chewing grass or just standing around looking very bored.

On this day, however, the two horses we saw were *extremely* close to the fence…They were also… uh…vigorously enjoying each other's company. My eyes bugged out, but I purposely didn't say anything aloud since I didn't want to draw any unnecessary attention to it. However, I heard a gasp come from the back seat and knew Harper had witnessed the gigantic gyrations.

"Whoa!" Harper exclaimed. "Dad, look at them!"

"Look at who?" I turned my head back and forth quickly, pretending not to see the love act.

"Over there, Dad!" he hollered – and pointed toward the horses.

I was forced to look where he pointed. (Not only was I amazed by the impeccable rhythm being displayed, I was also impressed by another "display" and it was suddenly clear to me why someone invented the phrase, "Hung like a horse.") Mercifully, we crested a hill and lost visual contact. I assumed that meant the discussion was over. However…

"What were those horses *doing*?!" Harper asked after a few seconds.

(What I thought at that exact moment was, "Son, those horses were DOING *the nasty*" but thankfully that's not what I said. I had something much better prepared.)

Me: "Uh…Well…Ummmm, Harp… I'm not exactly sure what was happening there."

There was an awkward silence that lasted about ten seconds and then Harper chuckled, "Oh - I get it, Dad. I know what they were doing!"

"You do?!" I gulped and gripped the steering wheel tighter.

"Yeah," Harper grinned. "They were *horse-back* riding!"

While witty Harper is thriving in 3rd grade and running us in circles driving him to *every* sport practice imaginable (with the exception of horseback riding, interestingly enough), Canton started 7th grade.

But before I discuss what having a TEENAGER has meant for our family, I want to relay a story from the spring, when Canton was finishing up 6th grade and he still thought his parents knew something….

Canton looked troubled one night at dinner, so Rana asked what was wrong. He said that he didn't really like his girlfriend any more.

We were surprised by this – mostly because we didn't know he *had* a girlfriend.

"How long have you been dating?" I asked.

"Almost the whole school year."

"Hmmmmmmm," I said, "Ok, so what's wrong with her?

"Nothing. I just like her as a friend," he said. "How do I dump her?"

"Well, your ole' Dad has had quite a bit of experience letting the ladies down," I joked.

He just stared at me.

I cleared my throat and said, "Well, how 'bout I pretend to be her, and you break up with me."

"That's just weird, Dad."

"Just try it," I said encouragingly.

"Ok," he said rather hesitantly.

Canton was silent for quite a while, then said, "Uh, Dad, I mean, Hannah, uh...I... I'd be happier without you. We need to break up." (Rana's face looked like the face of someone who had just witnessed a family of geese mowed down by a tractor-trailer.)

"Well, I like the *directness*," I said encouragingly. "But maybe you should be a little gentler - like maybe say something nice about her before you drop the brick pallet on her head." (Rana nodded emphatically.)

Canton tried again, "Hannah, you're still pretty. I have to dump you?"

"Better, but you're not asking her *a question*," I said. "How about something like, 'Hannah I think you're cool, but the summer's coming up and I was thinking it might be better if we were friends instead of being girlfriend and boyfriend.'"

Canton liked the idea. He repeated what I suggested: "Ok, Hannah, I think you're cool, but summer's coming and I think we should just be friends."

I slapped my wrist to my forehead and screeched in the most girly voice I could muster, "Oh the devastation! It hurts! I can't live without you, Canton!" I then I broke into a very realistic sobbing.

Harper giggled from his seat at kitchen table. Canton looked horrified.

"Do you think she's gonna *cry*??!! What do I do if she *cries*?!" he asked in utter panic.

"Well, I've had plenty of experience making the ladies cry." (Rana rolled her eyes.)

Canton said, "Dad, be serious."

"Sorry. Ok, just tell her you're sorry you hurt her but you still want to be friends."

Canton sighed, "There's *so much* I have to remember."

We practiced The Breakup much of that night. We practiced at breakfast. We practiced all the way to school. I had literally come up with 20 versions of Hannah's possible reactions and dramatic crying scenarios. We all even said a prayer together about The Breakup going smoothly (and without tears) before Canton got out of the car. He was a nervous mess as he headed into the building…

After school, I greeted him with, "So how did it go?"

216

"Dad, it worked *perfectly*! I told her what we practiced and she said, 'That's cool. I was thinking the exact same thing about just being friends.' And the best part was she didn't cry at all!"

Whew. Disaster averted.

That seems like it happened a long time ago, because Canton has now turned 13. That means we have a TEENAGER living in our home. Look up the word "teenager" in any reputable dictionary, and you will find the following definition: "Obnoxious." That is only partially true. We've also found "Rider of the upside-down emotional express" would be accurate.

Sadly, there isn't a self-help pamphlet out there to prepare parents for the psycho-science-experiment that goes awry when their child of 12 morphs into a true teenager. But I'm seriously considering writing a book about the transformation... I'd title it: "Why Are Our Friends Without Teenagers Always Smiling?" I even have a few ideas for chapter titles with broken-down sub-sections:

Chapter 1: Family Relationships:

*When a Pimple Ruins the Morning – for the Whole Family

*The Art of Remaining Calm: "I'm 13 and I Have Rights Too, You Know!" And Other Similarly Idiotic Teen Statements

Chapter 2: Hunger:

*I'm Soooooooo Hungry

*You Juuuuuuuust Ate

Chapter 3: Phone:

*Annihilating an Entire Month's Worth of Data Plan in Less Than 31 Hours

*Dealing With Death – When a Teen's Phone is Confiscated

Canton becoming a teenager also means he started middle school this year. This is a big deal. I've somehow survived working in a middle school for 17 years and I have a secret to share with all of you. Here it is: The general public has been tricked into believing that a middle school is a building where soon to be teens (and newly minted teens) go to get an education. This is not true. Middle school is actually a place where teens go to escape from their parents, socialize with their friends, stare blankly at their teachers, and criticize the cafeteria food.

You might not know this, but when the first school for 7th and 8th graders opened in 400 BC, it was called, "Looneyville." The government knew they had to step in and change the name to avoid mass hysteria. Thus, the more tame term, "middle school," was born.

I've taught at a "middle school" for so many years, I'm kind of numb to the insanity that goes on around me, but when Canton first walked into the building, I think he nearly went into shock. There's daily drama that carries on in the hall and seeps into the classroom. At first it all seems rooted in a logical plot line until you make the mistake of continuing to listen:

> *"Sarah called me ugly, so I told her I better not see her on the bus tomorrow. But – and you won't believe this – Jerry threw his pencil at me and said, 'Sorry, I almost popped you because you're a fat balloon,' but I don't care what he says, I love Jerry – he's sooo hot, even though Becca bought him a cheese pretzel yesterday at lunch and 'J' – that's what I call Jerry, I gave him that clever nickname, it makes him sound so cool like he is, you know? But anyway he is allergic to that cheese sauce, but my teacher told me Social Studies does matter in the real world, like how could I find the mall if I didn't know geography or if I wanted to buy Jerry - I mean, 'J' - a pretzel without cheese at the food court – but if I buy one, then I'll be fat and that would be bad because then I might break my phone if I sat on it."*

Canton didn't date that girl who was talking. I know this because then he would probably request that his mother and I refer to him as "C."

Truthfully, in 7th grade, Canton's luck with the ladies seemed to be trending upwards. An eighth grader told me a few weeks into school that there were 21, 8th grade girls who had a crush on Canton. I told him this, and he wanted their names immediately. I told him one name, but refused to divulge the other 20 – because I forgot them on purpose. Plus, 21 girls is far too ambitious a goal for a newly minted 7th grader. (Taking on *one* might be risky too!)

Then about a week later, Canton passed me in the hall exclaiming he had just gotten a girlfriend. I gave him a thumbs up. At the end of that same class, he passed by my room again and informed me that the girl had broken up with him via email. He said the relationship literally lasted 3 minutes.

Later that week, the same girl – apparently seeing the error of her ways – asked Canton out again. He said ok. (I questioned his judgment.) After 3 days, word on the street was that she was thinking about breaking up with him. (See?) So, naturally, *he* broke up with her in a lunchroom showdown before she could get around to it. This made her extremely mad – she called him "ridiculous" - and proclaimed that their friendship was over. Canton sent her a very nice email, and now they're friends again. (They might be engaged by the New Year?) Sorry if I lost you, but this is literally how Looneyville operates.

Side note: If you go into any home improvement store that sells dangerous equipment, you may see a sign hanging in the front that tells you how many days it's been since they've had an employee injured in a freak accident. The local Lowe's here is on Day #446. (I know in some weird way, I've just jinxed it, and the next time I go, the sign will read "Day #1.") Anyway, for many kids, this sign symbolizes life as a 7th or 8th grader. How many consecutive days can I go without having some kind of dramatic accident? Canton recently proclaimed he had three straight days of "girl free drama." (This may be a new Looneyville record!)

Since our descent into vicarious drama, I feel like Rana and I have been even more focused in Mass on Sunday. We obviously need God's help in raising these two guys. That is why it bothered me so much, one Sunday, to see Canton and Harper kneeling, butts shoved against the pew behind them and arms flopped like overcooked spaghetti noodles over the pews in front of them.

I looked at Canton, who was next to me. I nudged him, my eyes intently letting him know he should kneel a little more reverently – and with perhaps a bit more "straightness."

He kind of half-snarled, raising up one side of his upper lip. I didn't like that. I decided this was a perfect moment for a lesson. I nudged him again.

"What?" he grumbled under his breath.

I replied in a whisper through gritted teeth: "Take a little look around this church. Do you see *any* other person kneeling like a slobby mess in the pew like you are?"

He scanned each pew. (I smiled confidently.)

He kind of sat up straight and then leaned over to me. "That lady over there," he whispered.

I looked and saw the woman he indicated. I gasped.

"She's *at least* 102," I said.

"Well, she's *slouched*," he mumbled.

So when we got in the car to go home, I told both boys that next Sunday, I was done with the slouching... And, as a special bonus, I'd be asking them what the homily was about as soon as church was over. They bugged their eyes out in disapproval. (I bugged mine back at them because I am not mature.)

220

After church the next week, as we drove home, I looked in the rear view mirror and I asked, "Ok, what was the message that we were all supposed to learn today?"

Harper quickly: "That God loves us?" (He smiled widely.)

Canton: "Hey – he took mine. I was going to say that."

I looked at Rana. That had *indeed* been the message – in a loop-hole kind of way.

Over the next three weeks, their answers were eerily similar:

Week 2: "God loves us very much. "

Week 3: "We should love God."

Week 4: "We should love God because God loves us very much."

It was then that I stopped asking what the message was. ☺

Well, closing time… I want to mention that this will be our first year celebrating Christmas without Rana's dad, George, since he passed away in January. George was a great man – and no one ever had an unkind word to say about him. Maybe that's because George Bauer never had an unkind word to say about anyone else….We have no doubt he is up in heaven, chatting up the Good Lord on engine repair and Fords and probably wearing out the angels by constantly inquiring about what's on the menu for lunch when he just finished eating his last bite of breakfast. We sure do miss him….

George had a lot of sayings he shared with me over the years – but one of them might be my favorite. He used to say, "Take your time going, but hurry back."

The quote makes me smile when I think of George saying it and hopefully reminds us to soak in each precious step along the way and remember there are loved ones that will always be anxiously waiting for us to return home.

So this year, we hope you all cherish the tender moments with family, and allow yourselves to bask in the warmth provided by the blessings of those you love (even TEENAGERS)... We treasure each of you...

Love,

Us

EPILOGUE

224

Well, I guess this is where my first "book" officially ends... And hopefully, this is also the point where my second book begins – if having a teenager living in our home doesn't kill me...

This story is not truly over because the first installment of the sequel has already begun to be written – as our 2015 Christmas letter is nearly done... And, God willing, we'll have it and future letters to share with you years down the road.

Reliving the events chronicled in this book has left me smiling, and occasionally wiping a nostalgic tear or two away for sure. But mostly, it's left me feeling blessed:

Blessed that we've been given 18 beautiful years of stories to share...

And blessed that we've been able to share our stories with you...

228

Made in the USA
Charleston, SC
18 November 2015